MW01155334

Copyright, Legal Notice and Disclaimer

Table of Contents

Preface

Pretty much since the launch of Silhouette School Blog in early 2014, readers have been requesting a printable-format guide with tutorials in an easy-to-follow and logical order in an effort to get the most out of their machines.

While Silhouette School blog offers extensive tutorials, tips, tricks, and project ideas on using the die cutting machine and software, in some ways the blog is not conducive to certain types of information – nor is it terribly print-friendly.

All of these reasons have lead to the writing of "The Ultimate Silhouette Guide: Tutorials, Tips and Tricks to Get the Most Out of Your Machine."

I have poured as much information as I can onto the pages of this ebook – through written tutorials and photos/screen grabs - which can easily be viewed digitally and in print.

I hope you will find The Ultimate Silhouette Guide to be a one stop shop for everything Silhouette related.

Thinking About Buying a Silhouette? Let me Convince You!

Are you thinking about buying a Silhouette cutting machine? If you've been a crafter for any period of time you've probably come across a pin here or a blog post there that refers to a Silhouette.

There are currently four Silhouette America machines on the market: the original SD , the 12" die cutter the CAMEO, the CAMEO 2 (released in October 2014 with a touch screen) and the 8" cutter, the Portrait.

All of the machines are capable of cutting not only paper, but a wide variety of materials including vinyl, heat transfer vinyl, card stock, stencil material, contact paper, freezer paper, chipboard, adhesive-backed paper, fabric and more. The possibilities to create are only limited by your imagination and creativity.

Can it Cut…Make…Create?

Both the CAMEO and the Portrait can cut all the same materials as well as sketch, engrave, emboss (limited), create rhinestone templates, cut stamping material, and print and cut.

Materials that can be cut include:

Adhesive-backed Burlap Sheets
Adhesive-backed card stock
Canvas sheets
Card Stock
Cereal Box
Chalkboard vinyl
Chipboard
Construction Paper
Contact Paper
Corrugated paper
Fabric
Felt
Freezer Paper
Glitter Heat Transfer Vinyl
Holographic Heat Transfer Vinyl

Heat Transfer Vinyl (Smooth and Flocked)
Leather
Painters Tape
Scrapbook Paper/Printed Paper
Printer/Copy Paper
Printable heat transfer sheets for light and dark material
Stamping Material
Stencil Material
Vellum
Vinyl (Gloss and Matte/Permanent and Removable)
Washi Tape
Washi Tape Sheets

In addition, the cutting blade can also be replaced by a pen, pencil, marker, or chalk marker to create sketched designs.

There are also engravers on the market, most popular is the Amy Chomas Engraving Tip, that can be purchased to use with the Silhouette cutting machines.

A stylus is needed to emboss, although capabilities are limited due to the amount of pressure the motor on the machine can produce.

Portrait vs. Cameo

Which machine is right for you will depend on a few factors.

The two big differences between the CAMEO and the Portrait are the price tag and the cutting size capability. The Portrait is significantly less in size and price. However, if you can find a CAMEO Bundle on sale for under $230, the extra expense is well worth it for the larger size machine.

While the Portrait is smaller and less expensive, it is often difficult to find rolls of vinyl that can be fed into it without having to be cut down first. Cutting three inches off a 10 foot roll of vinyl is not easy to do in a straight line.

When the vinyl edge is not straight, there is a risk that it will not stay under the rollers and when it fails to stay under the rollers, the material slips and the cut malfunctions. There is a high risk of wasting a lot of material this way. That being said, 9" rolls of vinyl are available, though more limited. The Silhouette Roll Feeder is one great solution to preventing vinyl from slipping.

In addition, if you're a scrapbooker, scrapbook paper is 12x12 "standard. The 12" CAMEO is perfect for creating 12" scrapbook page layouts.

The other differences between the Portrait and the CAMEO are minor:

- With the CAMEO you have the ability to move the rollers in to account for smaller width materials. The rollers on the Portrait cannot be adjusted.

- The CAMEO also has a digital control panel while the Portrait has several different buttons, rather than a digital screen to unload and load the mat and materials.

- The Portrait is also smaller and lighter weight. It takes up less desk space and can be transported more easily, however, the size and weight differences should not be considered significant enough to really make a huge impact on a purchase decision.

Within the software, called Silhouette Studio, the Portrait and CAMEO have all the same capabilities. There are options you'll need to select on the Page Settings window (l) to pick which size mat (CAMEO or Portrait) you are cutting on, but the software will automatically detect which machine you have plugged in and will default to that page layout.

> My original machine was the Silhouette Portrait, the smaller of the two cutting machines. When I put the Portrait on my Christmas wish list in 2013 I was more of a DIYer than a crafter. I knew a Silhouette would take my DIY spirit and crafting to a whole new level, but I just wasn't sure if I thought the higher price tag was worth it. For a year I used my Portrait rarely feeling limited by the smaller size. However, a good deal ($199) on the CAMEO starter bundle pushed me to

purchase the CAMEO so I now use both machines, although admittedly I use the CAMEO more.

Once you've decided which size machine is best for you, consider purchasing your machine with a bundle. Silhouette America does a nice job of offering a wide variety of packages. Instead of only getting the machine, software, and 50 designs in your library to start, bundles offer more. Pick a bundle based on the main reason you are purchasing the die cut machine.

- If you are most interested in making vinyl decals, get the vinyl bundle that comes with some necessary tools and vinyl to get started.

- If you're interested in cutting fabric to make appliqués, purchase the cutting bundle that comes with the fabric blade and related items to get you started cutting fabric.

- If you're just not sure which bundle is best for you because you want to do it all, go for the Starter Bundle that comes with an extra mat, tools, and blades. You will always need these items when using your Silhouette machine.

Speaking of Essentials...

I'm often asked "Okay I have my Silhouette machine, what else do I need to go with it?" The bottom line is you'll need a blade (comes with all machines), a mat and your choice of cutting materials (listed on pages 6). Those are the bare bones essentials. It's a good idea to keep an extra blade on hand and rotate between two mats at all times.

While not absolutely necessary, the spatual (used to remove small paper pieces from the mat), scraper (used to burnish vinyl and transfer paper or transfer tape) and hook (used to weed vinyl and HTV) are almost impossible to work without; and will most certainly make the project easier.

The rest of the answer isn't so easy. It depends on how you want to use your machine. Throughout the book, at the beginning of each section, you will find essential tools and recommended supplies based on the material that's being cut.

Setting Up Your Silhouette

The first thing you want to do when you get your Silhouette machine is take it out of the box. Believe me, I've had more than my fair share of people tell me they've had their machine for months or years(!!) and they haven't even taken it out of the box. This thing isn't going to teach itself!

I know it can be overwhelming and intimidating and the lack of instruction does not help, but you have a powerful tool in your hand with *The Ultimate Silhouette Guide.*

The machine comes with a small getting started guide, a software CD, a USB cable and power cable.

Before you do anything, ensure you have fully unpacked the machine. Remove any and all tape and styrofoam that's on the machine being sure to open the cover and remove the tape that was used during shipping to keep the motor in position. If you do not remove this tape it can cause problems cutting, as well as causing a loud(er than normal) noise while cutting.

Plug the power cord from the machine into an outlet. Plug the USB cable into the machine. The USB end will connect to your computer. The computer and Silhouette must be attached in order to cut so consider this when you find a spot to set up the machine.

Once you've completely unpacked the machine and plugged in the cords, install the software CD on your computer.

The software that comes with the Silhouette machine is called Silhouette Studio. The current version is Studio V3. *You may hear users refer to Legacy or V2 which is a previous version of Studio that some users are still working with rather than upgrading to V3.*

If you ever misplace your Studio software CD and need to re-install you can download the most recent version of Silhouette Studio directly from the Silhouette America website.

The software CD will take you through a series of prompts to install the software on your computer.

Every machine comes with 50 free designs to start. However, after you install the Studio software for the first time, *your Silhouette Library will remain empty until you connect your machine to your computer using the USB port.* Close out of Studio and reopen. This will prompt the software to recognize your machine and your 50 free designs will be in your Silhouette Studio Library under "My Designs."

Don't skip registering your machine. It will not only activate the warranty, but it will allow your purchased designs to automatically download into your Silhouette library. Go to the Silhouette America website to register your machine.

Learn the Lingo: Common 'Sil' Terms

631 - Oracal 631 is the industry standard for indoor/matte/removable vinyl. It is meant for interior walls. It is adhesive backed, but not considered permanent. It's not meant for outdoors and should not be used on items that need to be washed or will be handled often.

651 - Oracal 651 is the industry standard for outdoor/glossy/permanent adhesive vinyl. It is meant for outdoor and permeant use and holds up well on items that will be in contact with water. It's still recommended to be hand-washed only. It is not intended for walls as it could peel the paint.

Compound path – The site on a design where two layers are 'compounded' or merged together to form a single one dimensional design.

Cut lines - Cut lines are the thick red or gray lines that are required on a design in order

for it to cut. Without cut lines, the Silhouette will not cut.

Cut lines are necessary for not only cutting, but also when using sketch pens. They tell the machine where to cut or sketch. When switched off or to "no cut" they tell the machine where NOT to cut.

There are several different cut line styles all accessible from the Cut Style window.

- Cut Edge: Indicated by a Thick Bold Bright Red Line around the edge of a design

- Cut: Indicated by a Thick Bold (but slightly dulled) Red Line on both the internal and external lines of a design.

- Perforate Edge and Perforate: Indicated by a Thick Dashed Gray Line around the edge of a design.

Decal - A design most commonly made from vinyl - either permanent, removable, or heat transfer. Depending on the type of vinyl used to create the decal, it can be placed on a wide range of surfaces.

Designer Edition – A one-time paid upgrade that allows the user to access more features and tools in Silhouette Studio.

Edit Points – Individual spots in a design that tell the edge of the design where to curve and move to form the shape. Edit points are used to manipulate the shape of the design.

Grouping - When two or more objects are put into a 'group' for the purpose of keeping them together while editing and designing. Overlapping areas will cut separately if they are not welded. Each object maintains its own cut lines.

HTV - Short for heat transfer vinyl...a type of vinyl that can be applied to clothing, apparel, bags, and hats with the use of heat - either a heat press or an iron.

Kiss cut - A cut made on a two layer piece of material - such as sticker paper or vinyl- in which the blade only cuts through the top layer, leaving the backing in tact.

Offset - An offset is the action of creating an equal distance border - at any distance of your choosing - around the edge of a design. Offsets are automatically welded in Silhouette Studio when possible. Offsets can be used to make a "background" or border for a design or text and even to thicken fonts for easier cutting. An internal offset creates an offset at the selected distance inside the design rather than around the outside.

PixScan Technology - A special cutting mat that allows the user to cut pre-printed materials or fabric by taking a picture and loading it into Silhouette Studio. The special mat keeps the actual proportions of the object using the PixScan technology.

Print and Cut - The process of creating a colored design in Silhouette Studio that is first printed on a home computer (or remotely printed at a professional-quality copy center) and then fed into the Silhouette CAMEO, Portrait or SD to be cut. Most often the cut line is only around the edge of the design and not into the detailed colored area. The use of registration marks is needed in print and cut.

PVPP: (Paint Vinyl Paint Peel) – A stencil painting technique in which the user paints a base coat, then applies a vinyl stencil, paints a second coat of a different color paint and then peels off the vinyl stencil. The color of the first coat of paint will show where the vinyl stencil covered the area.

Registration Marks: Essential markings that must be added to a print and cut design, before printing, so the machine knows exactly where to cut.

Reveal Grid – Exposing the grid lines, from the Page Settings window, on the work area in Silhouette Studio. Grid lines on the virtual mat correlate with grid lines on the Silhouette cutting mat to make placement of material easier and more accurate.

Reverse Weeding - Removing the area of the vinyl that would normally be left behind...most commonly used when cutting stencils.

Scraper – A tool to help smooth transfer paper, tape and vinyl when layering vinyl. Also used to apply and burnish decals.

Shear – A tool in Silhouette Studio Designer Edition that allows the users to slant the design or text by a certain degree.

Sketching - The same action as cutting, but

instead of using the blade to cut the material a sketch pen, pen, pencil or marker replaces the blade which causes the machine to sketch or draw an image or text. Silhouette Sketch Pen must be selected from the list of materials in the Cut Style window in order to sketch.

Spatula - A tool to help remove small pieces, usually of paper, from the mat.

Sticker - Different than a decal in that it's removable and made on paper-type non-waterproof material.

SVGs - A file format commonly used in graphic design. SVG files can only be opened in Silhouette Studio Designer Edition.

Trace - A function in Silhouette Studio which allows users to create cut lines around imported files including JPEG, GIFs, PNG, and PDF files.

Teflon - A sheet needed to go between an iron or heat press and htv to prevent the htv carrier sheet from melting. A thin piece of fabric - such as a pillow case can also be used if teflon is not readily available.

Text to Path - The process of manipulating text by curving it around another object such as a circle. When the text is converted to a path, it will maintain its new shape, even when the object in which it was wrapped around, is removed.

Weeding - The act of removing unwanted material around the cut design, usually using the hook tool.

Weeding Lines - Extra cut lines put into the negative space of a design to make removing the excess vinyl easier. This is done by cutting the vinyl into smaller sections to help with faster weeding, in addition it helps prevent the adhesive side of the vinyl from sticking to and ruining the design.

Welding - When two or more shapes or characters are formed into one solid piece with a single cut line around the entire shape. Welded designs will cut as one solid piece.

Work Area: The virtual mat area where designing takes place in Silhouette Studio.

Getting Started in Silhouette Studio

I have split this guide into four basic sections: Designing, Cutting, Materials, and Troubleshooting to guide you through pretty much any project you can imagine creating with your Silhouette. Since all projects start with designing in Silhouette Studio, that is the logical place to start here, as well.

Fonts and shapes make up the basics of designing in Silhouette Studio. By combining them and editing, you can create your own designs or modify existing designs found in the Silhouette Design Store, online, in dingbat fonts and elsewhere.

Purchasing from the Silhouette Design Store

Designs can be purchased from the Silhouette Design Store directly through Silhouette Studio (uu) or by going straight to the Silhouette Design Store's website (which often works better than going through the software).

Once you are in the store, sign in and search for designs by category or keyword using either the search box or the filter tabs in the blue bar along the top.

To purchase, click the design > click "Add to Cart" > Click on your cart > follow the prompts to check out.

Designs start at $.99. Sale designs typically start between $.50 and $.75.

> **TIP: Don't forget to grab the free design of the week from the Silhouette Design Store which is released every Tuesday.**

When you purchase a design from the Silhouette Design Store it will automatically download into your Silhouette Studio Library the next time you open the software *as long as you have registered your Silhouette machine.*

Unless you purchase a commercial license, designs and fonts are for personal use only and can't legally be sold.

Designs marked with a "P" are specifically designed as print and cut designs. Print and Cut designs can be found by searching "Print and Cut" in the search box.

There are also several 'sketch fonts' available for purchase in the Silhouette Design Store, as well. These are fonts that are specific for use with Sketch Pens and will sketch a single line instead of an outline as almost all fonts will. *Sketch fonts are not meant to be cut since they are only a single line and will only produce a single slice-like cut line.*

Opening Designs From the Silhouette Library

To open a design from your Silhouette Library, open up Silhouette Studio.

Click on the Studio Library icon (tt) on the left sidebar and you will be taken to your library where all of the designs you have purchased and designed are stored.

There are several design folders. The two you'll likely be using the most are:

- **My Library Folder** -Includes the free designs that came with your Silhouette machine and all designs purchased and downloaded from the Silhouette Design Store.

- **My Designs Folder** – Contains .studio files you've designed and/or anything you've saved to your library including edits to purchased or free designs downloaded from the Silhouette Design Store.

> The "My Patterns" folder includes all patterns you have imported. The "All Designs" folder shows all designs in alphabetical order. "My Fonts" holds fonts you've purchased from the Silhouette Design Store (but not fonts downloaded and installed on your computer).

To open a design into the Silhouette Studio work area > click the folder it is in > double click the design.

It will open up in the Silhouette Studio work area. Now you're ready to start having fun with editing and designing.

Editing & Design Tools

Silhouette Studio is a powerful and fairly versatile designing program. Learning the in's and out's of it will give you full creative control. But don't expect to master Silhouette Studio in one sitting or one project.

Start with a single, simple project and learn how the tools work on their own and in combination with other tools. Build on your skills with each project and you'll gain confidence in your creating. Designing for almost all material types – with the exceptions of HTV and Print and Cut – is essentially the same. So you can create one design and cut it as a stencil, a vinyl decal, a paper piecing and so on.

To get you started I've labeled, defined and described how each icon in Silhouette Studio works. (The tool bars shown are for the Silhouette Studio V3 Designer Edition which is why there may be a few extra tools than what appears in your tool bar. All basic Studio tool icons are also in the DE version.) Single or double letters in parenthesis after tool names, throughout the book, correspond with the tool bar labels on the following few pages.

Some of the design tools – including un/grouping, scale, weld, align, offset, replicate and some of the modify functions deserve further explanation and you'll find full details on them throughout the book.

Tool Bar Labels & Descriptions

Top LEFT Tool Bar

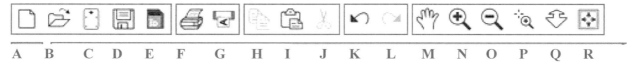

A New Window: Opens a new work area in Silhouette Studio

B Open File: Opens a file in Studio from the computer

C PixScan: Opens the PixScan window

D Save: Saves the design in the current work area; gives options to Save to Library, Computer or SD Card

E SD Card: Opens a window to access files saved on an SD card

F Print: Prints what is in the current work area that is within the printable area to the connected printer

G Send to Silhouette: Sends all designs with a cut line, in the current work space, that is on the virtual mat, to cut on the Silhouette

H Copy: Puts a duplicate copy of the selected design on the 'clipboard'

I Paste: Pastes a copied or cut design or text from the clipboard into the work area

J Cut: Removes the selected design and puts it on the 'clipboard'

K Undo: Undoes the last edit; can be hit repeatedly to undo a series of previous edits

L Redo: Reverses or 'undoes' the last undo

M Pan Using Mouse: Gives control to the mouse to pan around the work area

N Zoom In: Magnifies the current work area; Click repeatedly to zoom in closer

O Zoom Out: Provides a wider view of the work area; Click repeatedly to zoom out further

P Drag Over a Shape to Zoom: Click and drag over a specific area of a shape to zoom in

Q Zoom In and Out Using the Mouse: Use the mouse to zoom in and out of the work area

R Fit to Window: Fits the current work area in the window so the virtual mat can be completely viewed

Top RIGHT Tool Bar
(*Denotes Designer Edition Only)

S Fill Color: Opens the Fill Color window which allows the user to fill a completely closed shape with solid color

T Fill Gradient: Opens the Fill Gradient color window which allows the user to fill a completely closed shape with gradient color

U Fill Pattern: Opens the Pattern window which allows the user to fill a completely closed shape with a pattern. Designer Edition users can also import their own patterns (including pictures) to use to fill shapes

V Shadow*: Opens the Shadow Window giving DE users option to add shadow effects around designs and text

W Sketch Pen*: Gives DE users extensive sketch options for borders and filling

X Rhinestone Window*: Opens the Rhinestone window and gives options to turn regular cut files into custom rhinestone designs

Y Offset: Allows for an internal or external offset cut line to be generated around a shape

Z Line Color: Opens the Line Color window where the color of a shape's lines can be changed

a Line Style: Opens the Line Style window for selecting line styles including solid or perforated; line weight (necessary for lines to print on print and cut); end cap and line corner style

b Text Style: Opens the Text Style Window for selecting font styles, font size, justification, line spacing, and character spacing (Does not produce a text box in the work area)

c Move: Opens the Move Window giving full control over moving selected designs in the work space

d Rotate: Opens the Rotate Window giving options to rotate a select design by either a custom percentage or 45, 90, or 180 degrees

e Scale: Opens the Scale Window giving options to resize a selected design

f Shear*: Opens the Shear Window which gives DE users the ability to slant a design or 'italicize' a font

g Align: Opens the Align window giving the user the ability to align two or more shapes relative to each other or the work area

h Replicate: Opens the Replicate window giving the user the ability to duplicate designs in various ways; includes 'mirroring' options necessary for heat transfer vinyl designs

i Nesting*: Opens the Nesting tool which gives DE users the ability to put selected shapes into the smallest possible surface area to cut with as little waste as possible

j Modify: Opens the Modify window giving options to Weld, Crop, Subtract, Subtract All, Intersect and Divide designs.

k Trace: Opens the Trace window allowing imported designs to be traced to generate cut lines

l Page Settings: Essentially the control panel for the mat and cutting material – offering users the ability to indicate the size of the material being cut, the mat being used to cut on, and to change the page size of the virtual mat. Also where the 'Reveal Grid' controls are to reveal or hide the grid and numbers on the virtual mat; as well as the on/off for the printer and cut borders

m Registration Marks: Opens the Registraton Marks window to add registration marks to print and cut designs

n Grid: Turns on and off grid controls on the virtual mat

o Cut Style Window: Opens the Cut Style window where users:

- Select the type of cut lines for a select design
- Select the type of material being cut
- Find recommended cut settings
- Perform a test cut
- Send the design to cut on the Silhouette

p Send to Silhouette: Lets the user send the design(s) in the current work area to be cut on the Silhouette; Indicates status of current cut job

The V2 vs V3 tool top right bars are very simliar. However, there are a few changes in the icons that I think are worth pointing out for users still on V2.

1. **Cut Style** – In V3 this icon was replaced with (o)
2. **Page Settings** – Replaced by (l) in V3
3. **Offset Tool** – Replaced by (Y) in V3
4. **Registration Marks** – Replaced by (m) in V3

BOTTOM Tool Bar

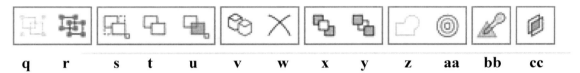

q   r   s   t   u   v   w   x   y   z   aa   bb   cc

q **Group Selected Designs:** Groups all of the selected designs or text boxes together so they move around the work area together

r **Ungroup Selected Designs:** Ungroups grouped objects so each can be moved independently; It may be necessary to 'ungroup' a design several times to fully gain access to all pieces

s **Select All:** Selects all objects in the work area

t **Deselect All:** De-selects all objects in the work area

u **Select By Color*:** Allows DE users to select all objects with either the same line color or the same fill color

v **Duplicate:** Makes another copy of the selected object

w **Delete:** Deletes the selected object

x **Bring to Front:** Brings the selected object to the front of other objects in the work space

y **Send to Back:** Sends the selected object to the back so it is behind other objects in the work area

z **Weld:** Welds two or more selected shapes or text characters together to form one shape and share a cut line

aa **Offset:** Allows for an internal or external offset cut line to be generated around a shape

bb **Transfer Property of Shape to Select Shape:** Gives the selected shape the same fill as shape that is clicked on with mouse

cc **Open Layers Pane:** Offers advanced layering design options

LEFT Side Tool Bar
(TIP: click 'ESC' to quit using the below drawing tools)

dd Select: Selects a design or text box when clicked on

ee Edit Points: Reveals the edit points of the selected design or text

ff Draw a Line Tool: Gives the mouse control to draw a line; hold down shift to make a perfectly straight line

gg Draw a Box Tool: Gives the mouse control to draw a box; hold down shift to make a perfect square

hh Draw a Rounded Box: Gives the mouse control to draw a box with rounded corners; hold down shift to make a perfect square

ii Draw an Ellipse Tool: Gives the mouse control to draw an ellipse; hold down shift to make a perfect circle

jj Draw a Polygon Tool: Gives the mouse control to draw a polygon free hand with a series of mouse clicks

kk Draw a Curved Shape: Gives mouse control to draw a curved shape; click around work area to create the shape

ll Draw Free Hand: Mouse turns into a pencil giving the user control to draw freehand

mm Draw Free Hand Smooth: Mouse turns into a pencil giving the user control to draw freehand, but edit points are automatically generated to smooth out the design

nn Draw an Arc: Gives the mouse control to draw a curved arc in any degree

oo Draw a Polygon: Draws a polygon; adjust the slider bar to change number of sides to as few as 3 for a triangle

pp Text Tool: Generates a new text box allowing the user to type in the work area

qq Eraser Tool: Allows the user to erase sections of a design (DE unlocks extra eraser features)

rr Knife Tool: Allows the user to slice or splice sections of a design (DE unlocks extra knife features)

ss Show the Drawing Area: Displays the work/drawing area/virtual cutting mat in Silhouette Studio

tt Show Library: Displays the user's Silhouette library in thumbnails and a series of folders

uu Show Online Store: Opens up the Silhouette Design Store where users can search and purchase designs

vv Show Library: Opens the library in the entire window

ww Show Library and Drawing Area: Splits the window revealing both the work area and the user's library

Grouping & Ungrouping

Most purchased designs and the free ones that come in the library will come into the work space grouped. You can tell they are grouped because they have one large box around all of the pieces of the design.

To move the pieces around, delete portions of the design, or manipulate individual pieces the pieces, need to be ungrouped. To do so: Select the design by clicking it > right click > ungroup.

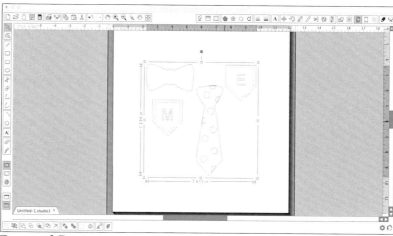
Grouped Design

You'll get several more boxes around the designs. However, some pieces of the design may be still grouped in smaller sections. Repeat the process to ungroup further (below right).

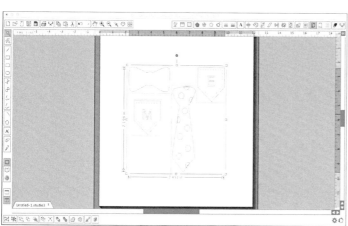
Ungrouped (Once)

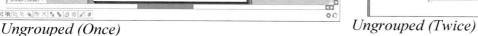
Ungrouped (Twice)

Delete what is not needed from the work space. To do so, select the piece by clicking on it, and hit delete on your keyboard **or** right click > delete **or** click (w).

If a duplicate of a design is needed: right click > duplicate or use the copy/paste tools (H, I, J) along the top bar or the keyboard shortcuts.

Welding VS Grouping

Understanding the difference between welding and grouping in Silhouette Studio is essential for working with designs and shapes and designing. In the most basic sense, grouping objects together forces them to move together while in Silhouette Studio, but has nothing to do with cutting. Even when grouped, each shape can keep its own cut lines.

Welding forms two or more designs into one design so they share a single cut line. Welding is necessary in designing when the user wants objects or text to share a cut line rather than cut overtop each other or individually.

Look at the example here involving the same shape. The left cross is "ungrouped" and we can tell this because each of the two rectangles has its own gray selection box around it.

The center cross is grouped, made obvious because there is one large selection box around the entire shape, but still each rectangle keeps its own cut lines (see how the red lines overlap each other?).

The right cross is welded (which automatically groups the pieces). We know this because there is just one solid cut line around the entire perimeter of the design.

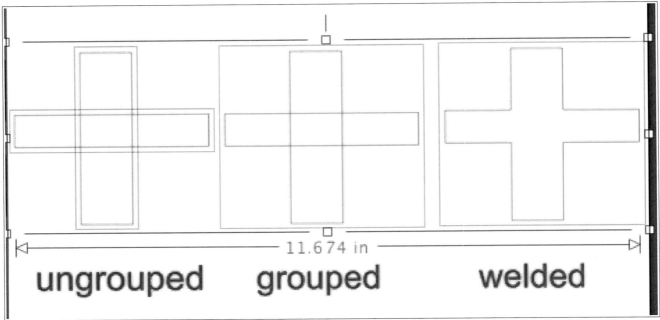

Grouping is done by selecting the individual pieces to be grouped at the same time > right click > group. Grouping is especially useful when needing to resize or move an entire design while also keeping it in proportion.

Ungrouping is done by selecting the individual pieces to be ungrouped at the same > right click > ungroup. Ungrouping is needed to gain access to individual pieces. However, not all shapes can be ungrouped due to compound paths.

Welding is done by selecting the individual pieces to be welded at the same time > right click > weld.

NOTE: Once text is welded or ungrouped it is no longer editable as text, but instead is treated as a design. For example, welded text will no longer be able to be put on a path or have the font style changed.

Also note, the only way to 'unweld' is to undo the action using the "undo" icon (K) along the top tool bar. Continually click undo until you get back before the weld. Keep in mind all edits and

18

actions that came after the weld will be undone, as well.

Resizing a Design (Scale Tool)

There are several different ways to resize a design. If you are working with just a single piece shape - such as the bowtie - you can simply select the design and do one of the following to resize:

1. Drag corner in or out watching the changing dimensions until you get to the desired size
2. Click the Scale tool and re-size by a pre-set percentage
3. Click the Scale tool and adjust the slider bar to a custom sized percentage
4. Click the Scale tool and manually type in the desired dimensions

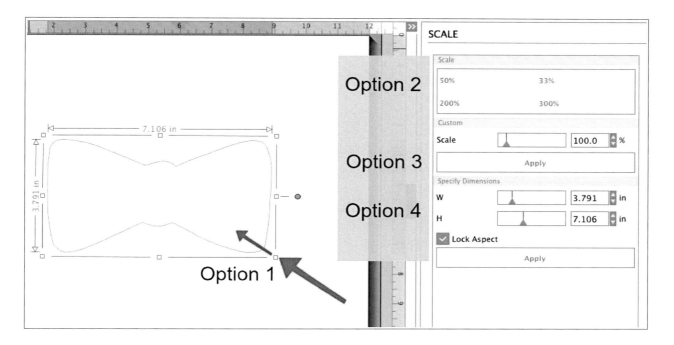

Unchecking the 'Lock Aspect' box will allow for full control over both the width and height of the shape, but will NOT keep the shape in proportion if the dimensions are not already such. For example, if a box is originally 4"x4" and the first dimension is entered as 2.5" and the second dimension is entered as 3.0 the square box will become a rectangle as the proportions are not being forced to stay the same as the original design.

Checking the 'Lock Aspect' box will automatically adjust the second dimension to stay in proportion after the first dimension - either height or width - is typed in. For example, if the box is 4"x4" and the first dimension is typed in as 2.5, the second will auto-fill to 2.5", as well, to keep the box in proportion.

Resizing a Multi-Piece Design

When working to resize a design with multiple pieces, it's likely, everything needs to be kept in proportion. Determine what size the design needs to be by measuring the surface where it will ultimately be placed. This could be a scrapbook page, a piece of wood for a sign, a shirt...anything really.

Once you have determined the size the design needs to be, begin the process of resizing it. Of course, you can use one of the four resizing methods explained on Page 20 for resizing a single piece design.

However, with a multi-piece design the fully assembled design is likely either wider or taller than any single piece. So to get a truly accurate measurement, it's best to quickly 'build' the piece in Silhouette Studio.

Based on the surface, determine if the height or the width is the biggest determining factor.

For example, let's say you have a Christmas tree with a stand and a star on top and some ornaments. To fit on the layout, the assembled design needs to be about 6" from top to bottom including the tree, stump, stand, and the star.

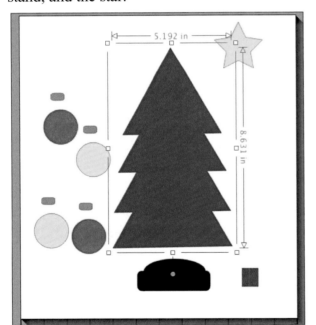

After ungrouping and by selecting just the tree, it becomes obvious that the tree alone is more than 8.5" in its original sizing (left).

If just the tree were resized down to 6" that would not account for the star, stump or stand nor would it resize those three pieces in proportion to the tree.

But by moving the star, stump and stand into place (the placement doesn't have to be exact) it's possible to get a good rough estimate of the fully assembled design's dimensions. Select around the entire design now and you'll see it actually measures more than 11.5" inches (next page).

Moving the ornaments into place is optional since they will not affect the height of the design. Just be sure they are *no higher or lower than the top-most or bottom-most* part of the tree. Leaving them within the height of the tree ensures they don't impact the height of the entire design.

To resize the entire design, select around all of the shapes with a large sweep of the mouse -including the ornaments so they are resized in proportion too. Now you can see the design is still just over 11.5" (right).

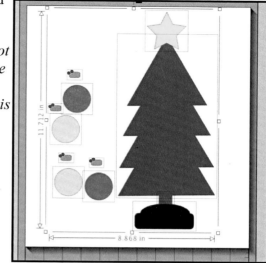

The width is measuring more than 8" - but we know that's not actually accurate because it's including the distance from the tree to the ornaments and the space between the ornaments. Since we are more worried about height and not width for this design, pretty much ignore that number.

With the entire design selected, grab one of the corners and pull the design in watching the height dimension along the side adjust as you go. Stop when you get to 6" - or whatever height you need to fit your space. (below)

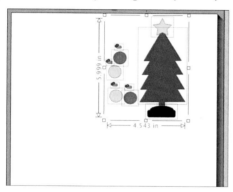

Another option instead of dragging in the corner to resize the entire design is to:

Select the Design > Group design > Click the Scale tool (e) > Check the 'Lock Aspect' box > manually type in the height dimension > apply (below).

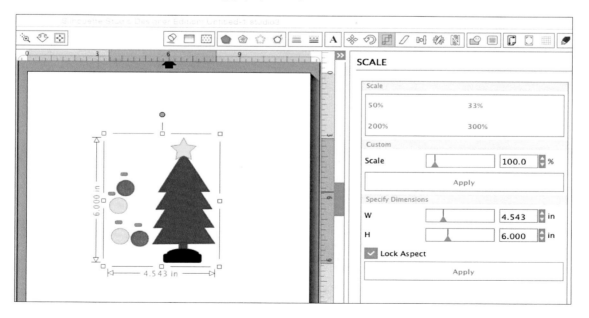

21

If the width of the design, in this case a tree, was the biggest determining size factor, the ornaments (or any pieces adding to the width of the design) would need to be moved into place on the tree since they will increase the width of the design. Anything that will increase height would just need to be within the width parameters (but not necessarily in place) before resizing.

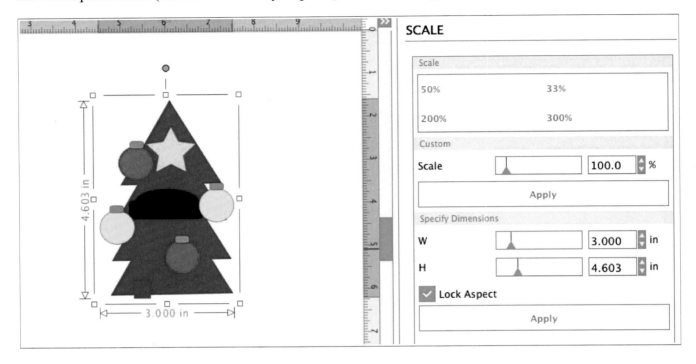

Align Tool

The align tool offers several different options for aligning a design or parts of a design. Using it means you don't have to 'eyeball it' and hope the design or text is centered.

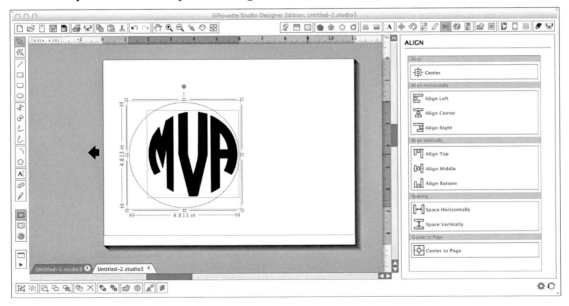

To get one design exactly in the center of another and evenly on all sides, make sure the 'inner' design (a three letter circle monogram in this example) is completely grouped. This way it is treated as just one shape and not three.

Move the group into the shape where it needs to be centered – a circle here.

Select both the inner and outer designs. From the Align tool window (g) click the very top option "Center." This puts the monogram exactly in the middle of the circle.

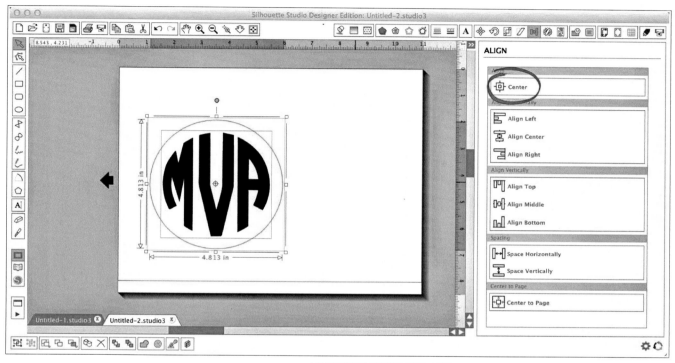

NOTE: The reason it's important to group the inner design is because if you don't, the software centers EVERYTHING putting letters perfectly on top of each other in the center. (Illustration 1)

Aligning top, bottom, left and right are pretty self explanatory, but aligning horizontally center and aligning vertically middle can cause some confusion.

Illustration 1

Aligning a group of words or designs "horizontally in the center" means the middle of all of the words or designs will be centered on the vertical axis.

If text is typed in a single text box, the text tool's justification (left, right, center) will align the text.

But if there is a group of words, each with its own text box, it is necessary to select each of the text boxes and then from the Align window > click the "Align Horizontally > Align Center" option to line them up as shown here.

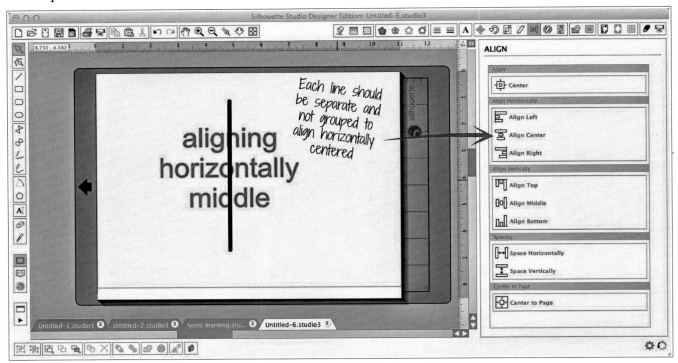

If you have a horizontal row of words that needs to be aligned, so the middle of all of the words are all lined up exactly, they'll need to be aligned vertically.

Select all of the words and from the Align Tool Window > click "Align middle" (from the Align Vertical pane). This will move all of the words on the same horizontal axis. In this case clicking 'align top' or 'align bottom' would have given us the same result.

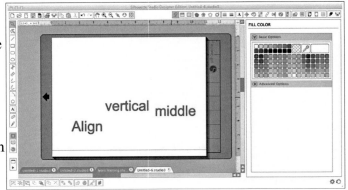

But there's only one problem..you'll notice that in this example, after being aligned vertically, the words 'Align' and 'vertical' are closer together than the words 'vertical' and 'middle' as shown here.

To make the words evenly spaced, keep them all selected and click "Space horizontally."

You'll see that 'vertical' is shifted slightly to the right, but is still perfectly aligned on the horizontal axis.

One final note, Center to Page puts whatever is

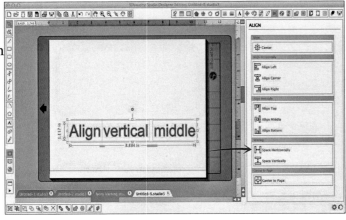

selected in the exact middle of the work area. Just be sure everything is grouped properly before this action is done or you'll have a big jumbled mess centered right smack in the middle of the work area.

Offset Tool

Offsetting is making an exact copy of the cut line – either slightly larger or slightly smaller (internal offset)- than an original design. The Offset tool (aa) is very useful for layering, cutting slightly outside the border on a print and cut, creating frames, thickening thin fonts that would otherwise tear when cut, and filling sketch pen fonts. Offset lines automatically weld any overlapping cut lines.

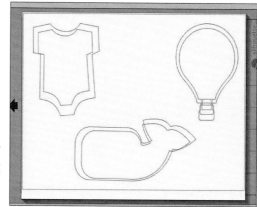

If you want to make two copies of the same design to layer on top of each other, you'll notice that copying and pasting and then enlarging one of the designs fails to make them line up correctly since they don't stay in proportion as shown here.

Instead, you want to use the offset tool to get an accurate border. By doing so the software will perfectly replicate a cut line either on the outside or inside of the original depending on if you pick 'offset' or 'internal offset.'

You choose the distance of the offset, as well....so if you choose a distance of .25 the cut line of the offset will be exactly a quarter inch from the original all the way around the outside of the design.

For this example, the original design has been filled with blue to show that the outer line is the offset line.

An internal offset would put the offset line inside the original cut line as shown to the right.

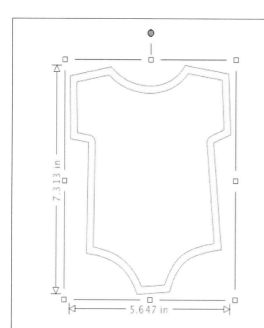

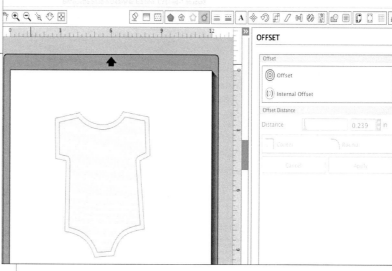

25

If both the original cut line and the offset line are selected at the same time and made into a compound path (Select > right click > make compound path) a frame is created.

Compound Paths

What are they anyway? And why do I care?

Compound paths are not an easy concept to explain, visualize or understand and therefore they are often confused with grouping and welding.

Making and releasing compound paths, however, are totally different than grouping, ungrouping and welding - and equally (if not more) important when designing in Silhouette Studio.

There are a few BIG reasons it's important to understand how compound paths work in Silhouette Studio.

- Compound paths influence how a design is filled with color, therefore are important for print and cut designs.
- Compound paths limit the designer's access to sections or pieces of a design so releasing compound paths becomes important when manipulating shapes.
- Compound paths make it possible to weld into a frame.

When you think of compound path just remember it means the lines or pieces of a design are "compounded" into a single layer.

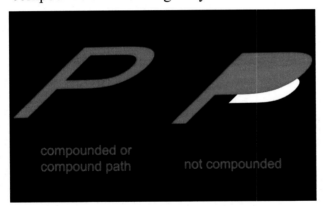

For example, let's look at the letter P. The letter P is actually made up of two layers: 1) the main part of the letter and 2) the counter. (Counters are the inside of letters such as P, A, O, D). The P in its regular form (left) is a compound path because the two layers are compounded. When a design is compounded (or made into a compound path), there is a hollowed out area at the compound site.

But if the compound path is released, as shown in the P on the right, the single layer letter will become two separated layers: 1) the main part of the P and 2) the counter. *In some cases, after the compound path is released it will still be necessary to ungroup to be able to separate the layers.*

Why Compound Paths are Important in Print and Cut

Compound paths determine how a design is filled with color and it all goes back to that hollowed out effect.

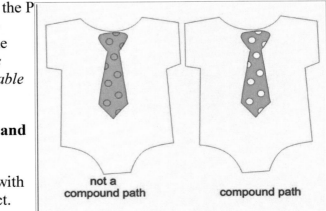

Let's say you have a tie design that you want to print and cut. If it's a solid tie you can simply fill it with color and the entire thing will print this way in the single color.

But if you want your tie to be on a white shirt and have white polka dots you want to make the tie and the dots a compound path. That will 'hollow out' those polka dots and essentially you'll be able to see right through the dot so you'll be seeing white of the shirt through the tie (right above).

Even if you do nothing but change the color of the shirt, the dot color will change as well. Again, because you're seeing *through* the dots. They are punched out.

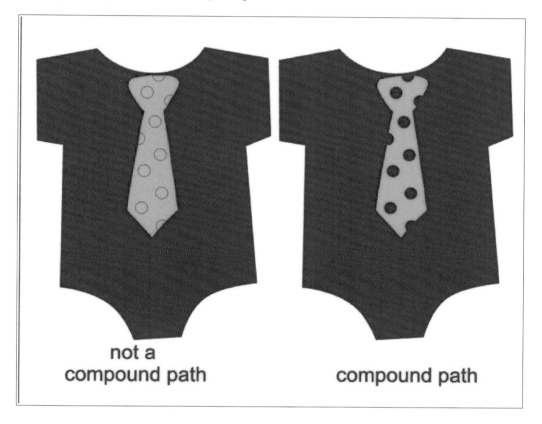

not a
compound path

compound path

But what if you want the polka dots on the tie to be a different color than the tie *and* a different color than the shirt? In that case, you need to release the compound path (select > right click > release compound path) between the tie and the dots.

compound path
released

compound path
released

THEN select ONLY the dots and fill them with a new color (right above).

At this point, it's a good idea to group everything together so it all stays together. If you attempt to make it a compound path again you'll lose the different colors because the paths will once again be 'hollowed out.'

Compound Paths and Manipulating Shapes

Compound paths are also important because they give you access to every piece in a design, as we've touched on with the counter of the P and the dots in the tie. Without releasing the compound path, you cannot gain access to either - even ungrouping will not work. That's because, as was discussed in the grouping vs welding section, grouping is simply moving layered pieces together so they stay in the same relative spot, while forming a compound path is literally joining the shapes together to form one new shape while still keeping their own cut lines.

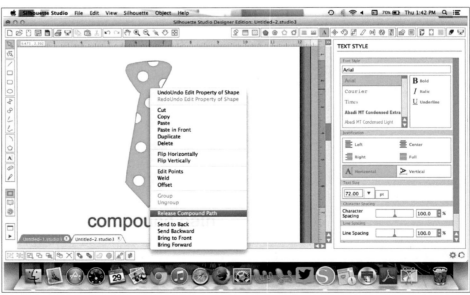

Since this tie is a compound path, if I right click on it I am not even given the 'ungroup' option. That's because it's not a group - it's a compound path.

If I release the compound path, however, the 'hollowed out' areas of the dots disappear and the dots take on their own layer to the design which allows me to move them away from the tie shape and/or manipulate them to my liking.

Compound Paths and Welding into a Frame

When you make a compound path you are essentially creating a frame. Just as a picture frame is hollowed out in the middle, so is a compound path. In order to weld into a frame you must make it a compound path first.

Let's use these two rectangles as an example. Right now it looks like you have a black frame around a red rectangle.

However, if the two boxes are not a compound path, the below image is what you actually have: just two boxes layered on top of each other. This is best demonstrated by slightly moving the top box so you can see the boxes are not 'hollowed out' into a frame.

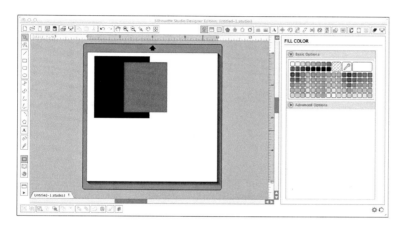

If you make the two boxes a compound path by: putting them on top of each other > selecting both designs > right click > make compound path, you'll get this...which is a frame! (The white is not a white box but a 'window' that you can see through.

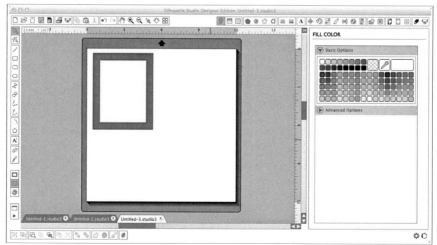

And since it's a frame, you can weld other shapes and text into it like in this example.

If the frames were not made into a compound path before the words were welded, the result would be an outline of the outer box only.

In that case, the software is being told to weld the text and inner box into the outer box which essentially makes them disappear since they are smaller.

Where to Find Designs (Other Than the Online Store)

Now that you have an understanding of how to work with and manipulate the very basic designs – those purchased from the Silhouette Design Store - you can move on to tackle designs from alternative places.

The beauty of Silhouette Studio is the Silhouette Design Store is just one place users can find and purchase designs. While the Design Store is the only place you will be able to purchase .Studio files, the software can open JPEG, GIFs, PNGs and, with Designer Edition, SVGs and PDFs.

Here are 10 places to look for designs that can be used in Silhouette Studio. This is certainly not an exhaustive list, but it is a good start.

It's also important to realize that most files imported into Silhouette Studio will need some actions taken to be cut including tracing or adjusting the cut line settings.

Google Search - Google image is a great place to start your search. Just a few key words and you can usually find something that will work for the design you're looking for. Any JPEG, PNG, or GIF can be brought into Silhouette Studio and traced to be made into a cut file which means the possibilities are pretty much endless!

PicMonkey - Picmonkey.com has a huge selection of free fonts, designs, labels, decals, shapes, and overlays that can be used to make a custom design or as standalone designs. There's a huge assortment of free designs, but you can gain access to all of the designs and fonts by upgrading to the Royale package for just $33 for the year.

PicMonkey designs are great for both print and cut projects as well as cut files - just save a jpeg

30

and bring into Studio to trace.

Dingbat Fonts - Dingbat fonts are a great resource for finding all kinds of designs! Since Studio accesses all fonts downloaded and installed on your computer and automatically turns them into cut lines, Dingbat Fonts are essentially a huge library of free cut files. An Internet search for 'dingbat fonts' or looking through font websites, like DaFont.com, and you can find dingbats for pretty much everything - Disney, Star wars, floral, animal, holidays, baby themes...you name it. Do a search for "___keyword____ dingbat font" and you'll be surprised at what comes up! Remember the upper and lower case letters often give you different designs.

Coloring Books - If you're looking for kids designs, coloring books are a great place to start. With their solid black lines and large designs you can easily scan a coloring book page and then trace it in Studio.

Pinterest - A search on Pinterest for "Free Silhouette Cut Files" brings up hundreds of designs that can be download and used in Studio. These are great because there's no tracing involved...just download, open and cut! Be sure to check out Silhouette School's Pinterest boards for free designs, too!

Silhouette Online Store FREE Shapes - Every week the Silhouette Online Store offers a free design of the week. During special promotional period, there are sometimes even more free shapes offered.

Design Your Own - If you're looking for something specific and it has some basic shapes you may be able to design your own cut files. This is especially true with text. There's no reason to *buy* text shapes. Ever! Instead of typing out a phrase in one solid line, make each word a new text box so you can easily move and manipulate the pieces of text. Make them different sizes and mix fun fonts together until you find a winning combination. The same goes for simple shapes like a bow tie: 2 triangles and a circle welded together; Mickey Mouse's head is just three circles, etc.

Change & Borrow from Designs You Own - Use the designs that you currently own in your design library as a starting block. Working with edit points gives you full control over the design. A baby boy's overalls can easily be turned into a little girls dress with just a few clicks of the edit points.

When you are buying designs, look for those with lots of separate pieces so you can ungroup them and use the elements separately, too.

Blogs - Craft and DIY blogs are always sharing free Silhouette Cut Files. It's kind of like a 'thank you' for reading and also a way to encourage you to come back! Be sure to check your favorite blogs often for free cut files - they'll often have a tab near the top of the page where you can find them all in one spot.

Silhouette School Free Files – Silhouette School offers free cut files so you can craft right along with me! Be sure to check out the Free Studio File section to grab all the designs I've offered.

Please keep in mind copyright laws and licensing when using Studio Cut Files and images found online. Most images can be used for FREE personal use only...but if you plan on selling products with an image or even a font on them you need to check on the licensing. This includes fonts and designs found in the Silhouette Online Store.

Now that you have a whole bunch of awesome places to find designs, many of them free, you need to know how to turn them into cut files.

Edit Points

Knowing how to manipulate designs you already own can be extremely beneficial. Edit points are the building blocks of every design and text. Knowing how to move, add, and delete edit points when designing will give you a huge advantage.

Edit points are those little gray or white or sometimes red circles you get all over a design if you double click the shape or text. You can also access them by selecting the design and clicking the Edit Points tool (ee). This also opens the Point Editing window on the right side. This is one of those 'hidden' windows that you can't just click on from the toolbar.

Let's say you purchased a design for a pair of boys overalls. By adjusting the edit points, you can actually turn them into a girl's dress in just a few clicks. Select the design and then click on the edit point you want to adjust. You can either drag it into position with the mouse or you can click the edit point, until it turns white, and click "delete".

In this example, deleting the center point between the legs (1), will force the two edit points on either side to form a straight line – like a dress instead of pants (2). Selecting the lines around the neckline and clicking "Make a Curve" will make the lines between the points curved instead of straight (3). You'll notice I've also manually moved in the edit points near the armpit area to make it a little more 'girly' (3).

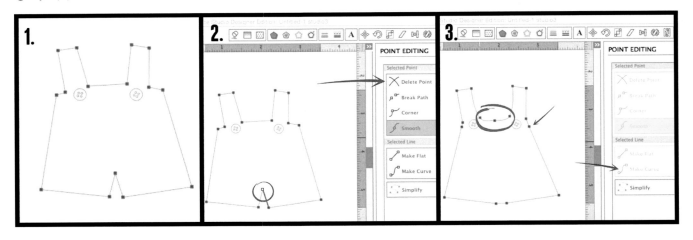

Hold down shift to select several edit points at the same time.

"Break Path" will create a break in the design. The break - as tiny as it is - is indicated by a red edit point. If you have a break in your design you will not be able to fill it with a color or pattern.

To repair the break and close it up, double click on the red edit point. The white dot with the gray line indicates the repaired break point.

Tracing: Converting JPEGs into Studio Cut Files

The first step in working with images from alternative sources is to save the design or image to your computer. Once you have saved a JPEG, GIF, or PNG file or image on your computer you can bring it into Silhouette Studio to cut it or create a print and cut from it. These are images that perhaps you found through a Google image search, a personal photo, or your company's logo or branding.

You do not need Silhouette Studio Designer Edition to do this (with the exception of SVGs and PDFs),

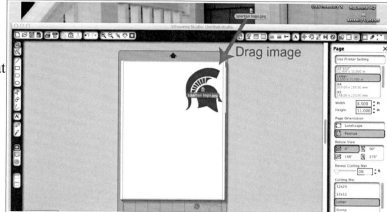

but please remember licensing rules. Images found online and elsewhere can, for the most part, be used for personal use, but if you plan to sell make sure you have the proper commercial license or that you are using a royalty free commercial image.

First, open Silhouette Studio.

Save your JPEG/GIF/PNG image onto your computer's desktop.

Simply drag the image into the Silhouette Studio work area.

TIP: It's easiest if you move your Silhouette Studio window so it's not taking up your entire computer screen.

Sometimes the image will come into the work area extremely large. If it does, use the Zoom Out tool (O) to zoom out so you can grab the corner selection box and resize.

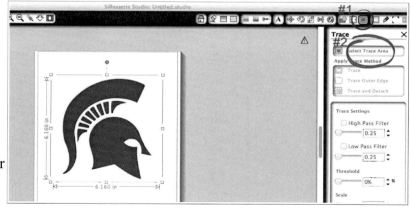

Click the 'Open the Trace Window' tool button (k).

Click 'Select Trace Area' on the right sidebar.

Using your mouse, draw a box around your image. A gray box will appear over the image resulting in some yellow outline lines.

Uncheck the 'High Pass Filter' box and slide the 'Threshold' bar towards the right. You're looking to get a nice clean, even yellow fill.

Click 'Trace' (or one of the other Trace Methods explained below) from the 'Apply Trace Method' pane and you will get a thin red line around the shape. Those are the cut lines.

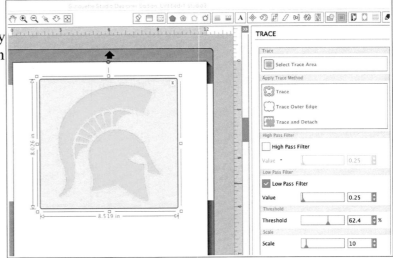

Trace Methods Explained

- **Trace**: Traces inner and outer lines of the image; Image with high contrast colors results in a better trace.
- **Trace Outer Edge**: Will trace only the outer edge of a design.
- **Trace and Detach**: Traces the outer edge of a design and detaches the original jpeg from the background. Great for use with print and cut

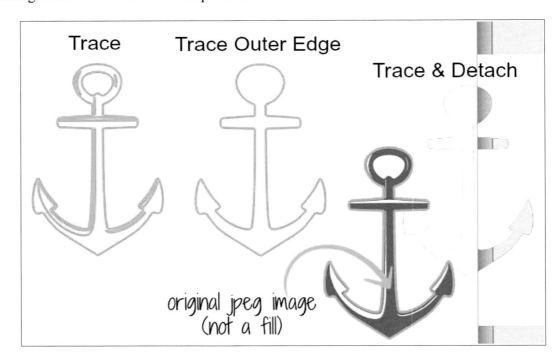

After the trace is completed, use the mouse to grab the original colored image and pull it out of the work space. The trace/cut file will stay.

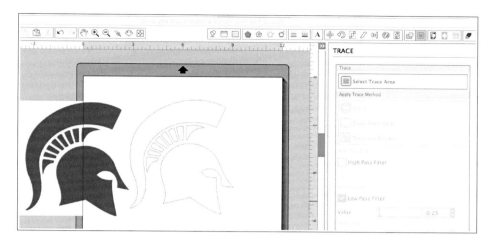

Click on the original JPEG or GIF image and delete it – you do not need it any more (unless you are making a print and cut). You should be left with only the cut lines.

After cut lines are generated, it's easiest to 'see' how a design traced by filling it in with color using the Fill Color tool (S).

Manipulating Traced Designs

To separate and gain access to individual pieces of a traced shape (to add color, change line color, delete, move, etc) you will not be able to simply right click and ungroup.

Instead, the image's compound paths need to be released: Right click > release compound path. When the paths are released you can then group smaller sections of the design together and make them compound paths. This will allow for filling with different colors or patterns using the fill color or fill pattern tools.

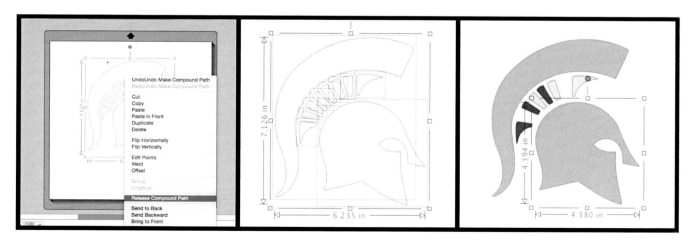

Tracing Photos

Tracing photos is different than tracing other types of designs and images, although the trace tool (k) is still used. It is important to pick the right photo to trace. Look for a photo that is high in contrast and does not have busy background.

Since the tracing function works on finding contrast between colors, it's easiest to trace a black and white photo so if you have a color picture, convert it into black and white using a free program such as PicMonkey.

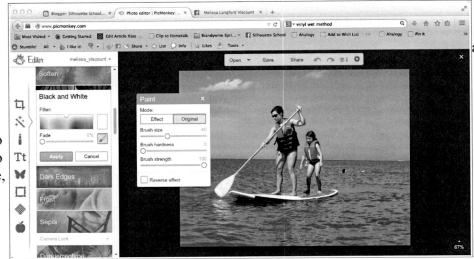

Go to PicMonkey.com >
Click 'EDIT' > navigate to your photo. Once the photo is open click on the icon along the left side that looks like a wand with some stars (in blue along the left side). Scroll down until you find 'black and white' then click Apply.

Still in PicMonkey, click the very top icon (in blue along the left side) and pick 'Exposure'.

Move the bars around until the blacks and whites are pretty drastic. The contrast bar is a good one for this.

Save the photo as a JPEG or PNG and then reopen it in Silhouette Studio by dragging and dropping it into the work area as described in the previous section.

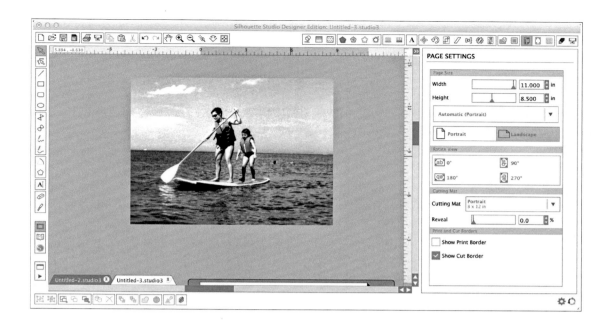

To trace the image, click the Trace icon > Click Select Trace Area > Select around the photo > TRACE (**keep high pass filter checked**!)

You'll have red lines everywhere and it will look like a whole big mess.

Move your trace off of the photo. Use the fill and line color tools to fill your image with black.

Half way there...but the original photo needs to be traced again.

Go back to your JPEG image and trace again. Only this time, you want to UNCHECK high pass filter and adjust the threshold.

Finish the trace by clicking 'TRACE' and again fill in the red cut lines with black fill and black lines. These are what your two traces look like.

Neither is perfect (although some may want to go with the second trace alone), but when the two traces are layered together, you get the best trace with the most detail.

So use the mouse to grab one of the traced designs and move it on top of the other. Zoom in and focus on one area so you can see exactly how to align the two traces. Once you have it perfect, GROUP THE TWO TRACES!!!!

Now you can print, print and cut, cut on vinyl, or sketch...there are so many options.

Turning a Photo into a silhouette

Perhaps you don't want your design to have so much detail, but instead prefer the silhouette look. This can be accomplished in Silhouette Studio, too, but the process is different. Instead of tracing, it's edit points that make the silhouette.

Drag and drop the picture into Silhouette Studio.

The photograph you pick is actually very important. You are looking for a picture that will still be recognizable just by the silhouette. Photos that are straight on are usually not good options.

Once you've found a good photo, get rid of as much background as possible. Use the knife tool (rr), as opposed to the eraser tool (qq), to make slices around the part of the image you wish to make into a silhouette.

Then use the select tool to drag the cut sections away and delete them.

Now you're ready to start dropping edit points around the photograph. Use the 'Draw a Curve Shape'

Tool (kk) to do this.

You can start anywhere, but it's easiest to start dropping points in the middle of the photograph instead of near the edge of the picture. I started at the top of the man's hair and worked down and around dropping points (clicking) every half centimeter or so - sometimes closer when there was a turn or curve and sometimes further away when there was a 'straight away' (as in at the bottom of the picture).

Be sure to pick up as many details as you can, that's what's going to make the Silhouette recognizable.

Once you have gone all the way around the photo dropping edit points the outline will turn red as shown in the picture below.

Zoom in really close now...

Click on the 'Edit Points' tool (ee) and adjust any of the points that need to be slightly moved in or out. For instance, in this screen grab you can see that the line is not very tight to the man's head on the right side or near his left ear.

I thought I was placing the edit point right on his hair line, but it was actually not exact so I just dragged those points in to where they should be as shown in the below image.

Again, go all the way around the image adjusting the edit points until you get back to where you started. Be sure to connect the first and last edit points to create a closed design.

Zoom back out and using the 'Select' tool (dd), grab the original image.

Move the original JPEG to the side to reveal the silhouette outline you've created. Delete the original.

To fill in the outline, click the 'Open the Fill Color Window' (S) along the top tool bar. Select the color you would like to fill with.

Now you're ready to print or print and cut your silhouette image.

TIP: If you are having trouble filling the shape with a color, it's because the outline is not completely closed. Double click the edit point line and look for the bright red dot - that's where the end is. Click it again to close the shape so it's fillable.

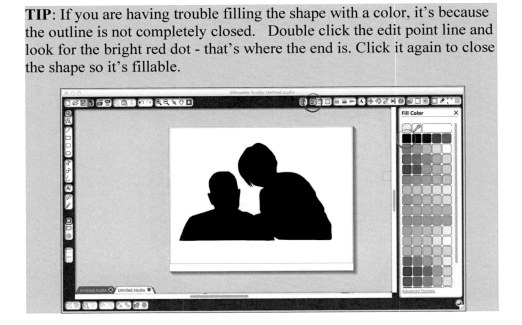

Creating Mock Ups

Mock ups are a great way to preview a design, layout or project before you actually create it. If you sell items you make with your Silhouette you may want to make mockups so you don't have to physically create an example of every single option - be it color, phrasing, size, personalization - you offer. There are a few different ways to go about making mock ups in Silhouette Studio.

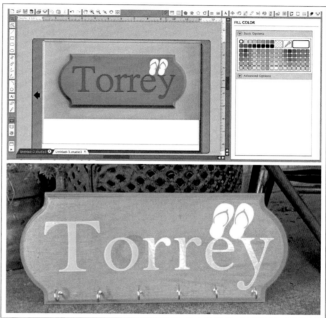

- For example, if you are making a sign with vinyl lettering or a stencil use the draw a box tool to draw out a box the exact same size as your sign. *You can also take a photo of the actual sign and import it into Studio and then size it to its actual proportions.*
- Use the Scale tool (e) to input the dimensions.
- Fill the box with the color paint you plan to use. If you're not sure what color paint or stain would look best make a few copies of the box and fill them with different colors or pick a wood grain from the Patterns Fill tool.
- Then add your text.
- Move the text on top of the box just as you would like it to be on the sign.
- Fill the font with color and change the line color to transparent so you can get a real sense of what the finished project will look like.

The Fill Color tool (S) is used to add solid color to a shape or text. To use it simply, select the shape or text, click the fill color tool and then pick a color. The Gradient Color tool (T) and Line Color tool (Z) are used the same way.

> TIP: Don't just wait for a print and cut design to use the fill tools. When designing any type of project, use the fill tools to help see what a finished project will look like. Play with color combinations in Silhouette Studio to avoid cutting materials only to realize after they're cut it's not the look you were going for.

Also, by filling shapes and text with color, you will be able to take advantage of some shortcut options such as "Select By Color" which selects all objects of the same color in the work area.

Mock ups can also help with layout and sizing. You can find more on mock ups in the Stencils section.

Silhouette Studio Designer Edition

If you're serious about designing or just want to give yourself some extra options, Silhouette Studio Designer Edition is worth the investment.

The questions surrounding Silhouette Studio Designer Edition are many...but the two biggest are: "Is it worth the price?" and "What is so different from the standard software that comes with the Silhouette machines?

NOTE: Upgrading to Silhouette's Designer Edition is NOT the same as upgrading from Studio V2 to Version 3. The V2 to V3 upgrade is a free upgrade that you can download from the Silhouette America website to get the new software.

The MSRP for 'DE,' as it's often referred, is $49.99, but you can often find the DE download cards on Amazon for around $32. It's a one time paid upgrade.

Once you purchase the Silhouette Designer Edition Upgrade Card, follow the directions on the back to enter the license key and registration found in the Help Menu along the top of Studio. When you open Studio it will automatically be the Designer Edition. Here are 13 added features you get with the one time Designer Edition upgrade.

Designer Edition offers a **wide range of Sketch Pen options** (W) that are not available with the standard software. Plus, there are ways to fill in a sketch design to make it look like pencil, charcoal, scribble and so on.

One of the biggest draws to Designer Edition is the **Rhinestone feature (X)**. With the click of a button you can turn any design into a rhinestone design. This is not possible with the standard software. Rhinestones come in various sizes and the DE feature lets you easily manipulate the size and layout of the rhinestones patterns.

DE gives you the option to put a true **Shadow** (Y) behind a shape or text.

The **Eraser tool options** (qq) dramatically expand with Designer Edition. Forget the single circle eraser, you can pick the shape and size of the eraser and actually use it to create cool designs and patterns. Plus, you can manipulate the eraser so the design stays open or becomes a closed shape which gives you twice as many design options.

Similar to the eraser tool, the **Knife tool (rr) is hugely expanded** in Designer Edition. Instead of a just a single straight line cut like in the standard version, the options are endless in DE.

The **Shear tool (f)** lets you move designs to all different angles either vertically or horizontally. This also gives you the ability to italicize fonts that don't have this editing option otherwise.

Have a design that's filled with various colors and now you want to group or rearrange them for easy cutting in the work area? Use the **Select by Fill Color or Line Color (u)** in one click. Very handy...and a big time saver!

One of the most helpful tools in Designer Edition is the **improved rulers and grid (n).** Turning on the grid you can change the size of the boxes to get a more exact measurement of your design. Instead of just the 1" square box, you're able to break those boxes down into quarters and eighths and smaller or larger.

The **Ruler tool** gives you a measurement that is much more precise than the ruler in the standard Studio software.

Nesting (i) - This is where the price of Designer Edition will literally pay for itself. The nesting tool will put the selected shapes into the smallest possible area without overlapping so you use the least amount of material to cut on.

The **Transfer Properties tool (bb)** lets the user

select a shape and transfer the color or pattern fill to another shape. Just click on the Transfer Properties button and highlight the shape and then use the eyedropper to click on the property you want duplicated.

Designer Edition also unlocks the ability to (much more easily) **fill shapes with photos** by using the My Patterns function.

Perhaps the biggest benefit is that Designer Edition allows users to **import SVG files.** Many designers sell and offer SVG files, but without DE they can't be used by Silhouette Studio users.

Working with SVGs

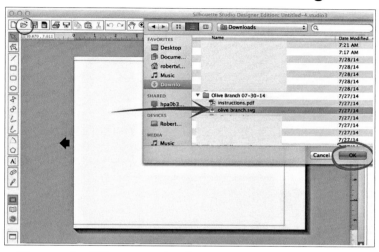

Lots of designers use and sell their designs in SVG format. SVG is a file type that allows for the image to be scaled without reduced resolution.

To open SVG files in Silhouette Studio, Silhouette Studio Designer Edition is needed.

To import SVGs into DE, simply click FILE > OPEN and navigate to the SVG file on your computer. (Make sure the file is unzipped if it was a zip file when you downloaded.) Click the file and it will open in Silhouette Studio.

Most likely the imported SVG will NOT come in with cut lines. This means if you try to cut the design, nothing will happen.

Cut lines are indicated by a red outline. To check if the imported SVG has cut lines, go to the Cut Style window (o). If there are not thick red lines around the image, there are no cut lines and you'll need add them.

Select the design > Click 'Cut' or 'Cut Edge" and everything will get a cut line around it.

If you click cut and still don't get cut lines you will need to trace your design using the trace

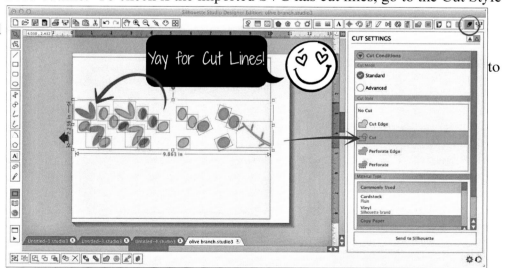

function to add cut lines; then delete the original image as was described in the cutting JPEG section.

Once you have cut lines you can manipulate (resize, re-color, delete, copy, etc) the design as you would like to before you send it to the machine to cut.

Opening SVGs without Designer Edition

If you're in a pinch and do not have Designer Edition, but you really need to import an SVG into Silhouette Studio, you can work around this by first converting the SVG file into a file type that Studio will recognize such as a JPEG, GIF, or PNG.

The easiest way to do this is to use an online conversion tool, like Zamzar, to change the file from SVG to JPEG. Simply go to ZamZar.com and follow the on-screen instructions:

- Step 1: Navigate to find your SVG file on your computer.
- Step 2: Choose the new type of file (JPEG) from the drop down list.
- Step 3: Enter your email address so the JPEG file can be emailed to you.
- Step 4: Click CONVERT.

You'll be sent an email with a link in it which you need to click to download your JPEG file.

The file will be downloaded to the folder or desktop where you assign it on your computer.

Now, as a JPEG file you can drag and drop this file into Silhouette Studio and trace the design to get the cut lines around it and make it into a cuttable design.

Despite the free SVG to JPEG workaround, I still say Silhouette Studio Designer Edition is worth the upgrade especially if you can find it on sale for around $30.

Fonts and Text

One of the best things about Silhouette Studio, as a design software, is that you can use any font downloaded on your computer in Silhouette Studio. There are literally thousands of downloadable text and dingbat fonts available - many of them for free for personal use.

The first thing you need to do to use a font in Silhouette Studio is to find one. You can do this in a few different ways:

- If you're **looking for something very specific**, say a Disney Dingbat Font, start with a google search. Type in something like "Disney Dingbat Font." Usually something on DaFont.com or FontSpace.com will turn up towards the top of the search query. You'll get a preview of the font there and you can either download or keep on searching.
- If you're **looking for a specific style** do a search on a font website. Start with DaFont.com because they break down their font styles. If you're looking for a Western-style font just click on that category and quickly scroll through the Western options to find what you want to download.
- If you just **need ideas of cool fonts** and awesome font combinations, do a Pinterest search for 'free fonts.' Keep a board of your favorite fonts as you come across them.

Downloading New Fonts into Studio

Be sure Silhouette Studio is closed while you go through this downloading and installation process.

Once you find the font you want to download onto your computer, click Download. It will go to the folder where you direct it to download.

Click the file to unzip it. Now you've unzipped the file, but the font is still not actually downloaded into your font book.

To actually install the font, click the name of the font followed by .TTF or sometimes .OTF.

(NOTE: Follow through the on screen prompts to install the font. The following steps work on a MAC)

Double click the font name and you're taken to yet another pop up window asking if you want to install the font. Confirm that you want to install and the installation will begin. And there's your font successfully downloaded, installed and listed in your font book!

Only after you've *downloaded and installed* the font should you open Silhouette Studio.

If you had Silhouette open while you were downloading the font, restart the program or the font won't show up in your font list.

The font will now be listed in your font list.

To access it, click the Text tool (pp) and type something.

A window will pop up on the right side to give you a bunch of different options for manipulating the text.

Start by picking your font. Remember, all fonts downloaded and installed before you opened Silhouette Studio during the current session will be available to you.

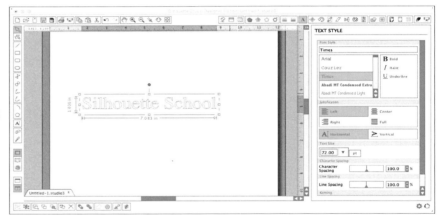

Select the line of text by clicking on it. Then from the Font Type pane click on a font name. The text will change to that font. In this example, I've changed from the default, Arial (above), to Times (below).

Using the arrow keys on your keyboard, arrowing down through the font list will change the font of the text in the selected text box. Once you find the perfect font, you want to size it.

Size the text by either selecting it and dragging the corner box in or out or picking a font size in the "Font Size" pane.

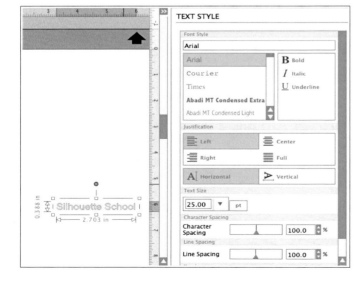

The distance between the letters can be adjusted by sliding the Character Spacing bar to the right or left.

The distance between several lines of text (that are within the same text box) can also be adjusted by sliding the Line Spacing bar.

To fill text with color, select the text and pick a color from the Fill Color tool (S). You may also want to change the line color by selecting the font > clicking the Line Color tool (Z) > picking a color.

Filling text with color is useful for printables, mockups, and print and cut.

TIP:
Text must either have a color fill or a line weight for print and cut or it will not show up when printed. Read more in the Print and Cut chapter.

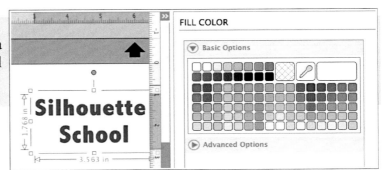

If you weld, ungroup, or release the compound path of a line or lines of text it will no longer be editable as text and will instead be treated as a shape or design. This means you will not be given certain options like changing the font style or converting the text to a path (wrapping the text around a circle). You can click 'undo'(K) to go back if you decide you do not like your edits.

For this reason, if you have several lines of text that need to be different fonts or font sizes, it's best to type them each out as new text blocks so you can more easily manipulate them.

Double clicking on text gives you the green box editor which allows you to make typed changes to your text.

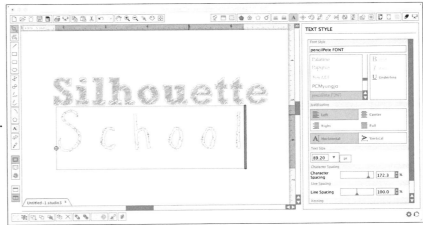

Thin Fonts

Some fonts are so delicate and thin that they are very tough and frustrating to cut. Don't get frustrated and give up on your favorite font if it tears while you cut it - there is a way around thin fonts even one as thin as Edwardian Script ITC.

Even in font size 72, the font is very thin in many areas. Cutting it like this on vinyl, and especially paper, would likely cause it to tear.

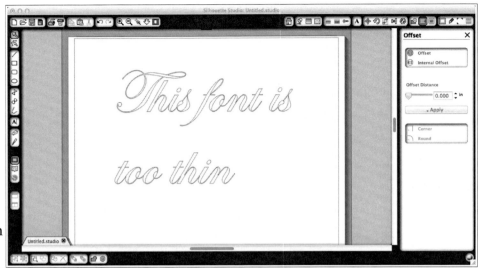

Many fonts can't simply be made 'bold' in Silhouette Studio. You can, however, use the Offset tool (Y) to increase the thickness of the font to make it easier to cut.

To do that, highlight all of the text (whether it's a single word or a sentence) and group it. (Highlight > Right Click > Group) This will help us out later. While the text is still highlighted click the 'Open the Offset Style Window.'   Click 'Offset'.

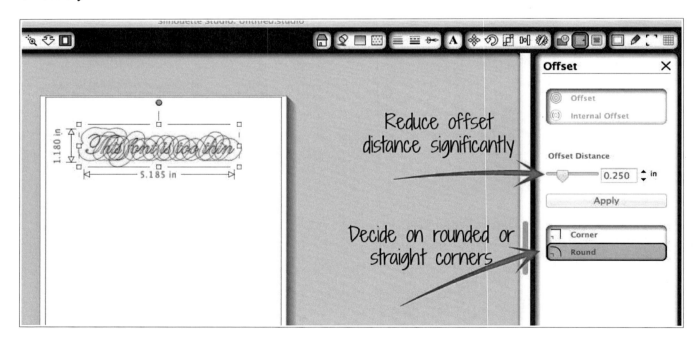

The default offset is .25" which is way too large for this font. You want the offset to be between .010" and .025" depending on the font. The offset needs to be pretty tight so the detail in the font isn't lost and so the letters don't start blending together.

If you make the offset distance too large, you may lose 'middle' areas of letters (called 'counters' like the 'f' and in the top of the 'T').

Select whether you want the offset to have rounded or straight corners. Here's how this text looked after the offset distance and corner adjustments.

If you look closely, you can see there is a slight outline around the original text...that's the offset that was just created.

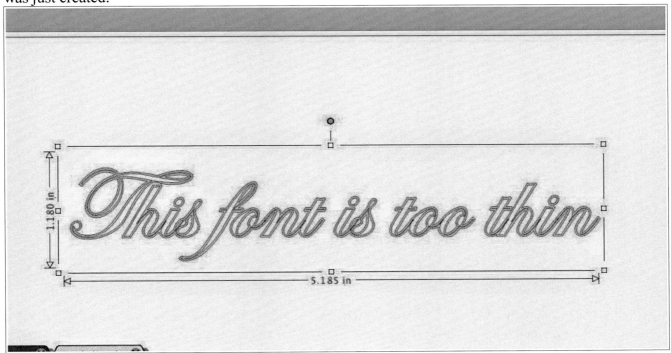

Once the offset is how you like it, you can pull the original text (top below) away and delete it. Just highlight it (this is why you grouped it) and drag it away from the offset. You'll be left with just the offset (below) as your cut. Can you see how the offset on the bottom would be much more Silhouette friendly?

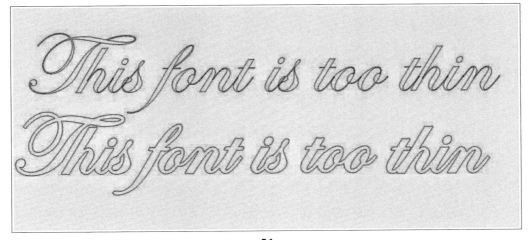

TIP: Grouping vs. welding - Grouping text will not have it cut as one solid piece since grouping is only a function of Silhouette Studio. Grouping allows the user to put several individual elements in a 'group' so they move around the work area together while each maintains its own cut lines even if the items in the group are overlapping. Welding on the other hand is when items are physically joined together so they cut as a solid unit and not individual characters or designs.

Welding Text

Some fonts can be easily 'welded' or joined together (think script) so that they'll cut as a solid or partially solid word instead of individual letters.

Type a word into your work area. If it's a script it may appear to be overlapping already similar to this font where there are areas of each letter that are overlapping.

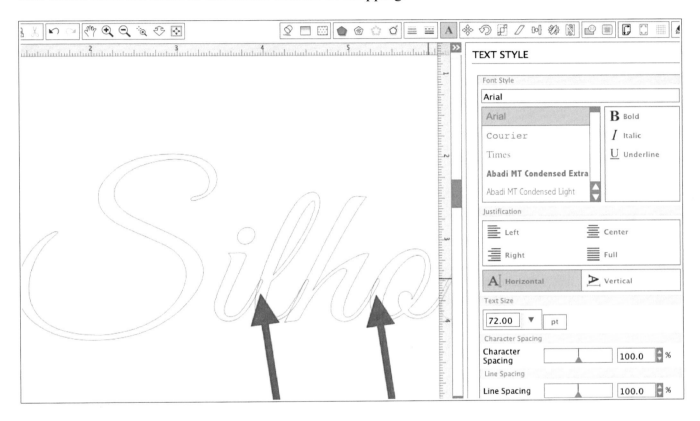

If you cut like this, each letter would still be cut separately since each maintains its own cut lines. For letters that overlap, such as the i-l, l-h, h-o you'll be able to weld or join them together by simply selecting the text > right click > weld or by selecting and hitting the Weld icon (z).

Notice how the letters have all welded together? Keep in mind the dot above the 'i' and the S are not welded to the rest of the word because no part of them was touching another letter when it was welded.

Numbers and non script fonts can also be welded. They just require a little more work.

To weld characters that are not touching you'll need to move them closer together.

You can do this by either using the character spacing tool (in the Text Style window (b)) or ungrouping and manually moving the characters until they slightly overlap. Select all of the characters > Right click > weld.

Now you have one solid cut line around the entire unit instead of individual cut lines around each letter or number.

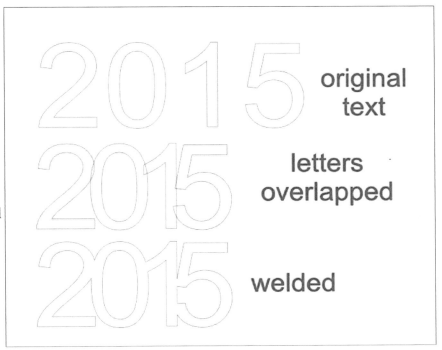

Once any of the following edits has been done, the font style cannot be changed since it will no longer be treated as a font, but instead as a shape:

- Text is welded
- The compound path has been released
- The text has been ungrouped

If you want to change the font, use the undo button (K) to go back as far as before the edit.

Text to Path

Text on a path is a fancy way of saying making text wrap around a shape. That does not mean making text form into the shape like word art, instead a line of text will take the form of a line such as a circle to make curved text or a roller coaster on a squiggly line.

If you're trying to make text curve around a circle - or along a squiggly line or around the perimeter of any shape - in Silhouette Studio you can do so in three simple steps.

Open Silhouette Studio and select the 'Draw an Ellipse' Tool (ii) to draw a circle.

Next, select the Text tool (pp) and type out the text.

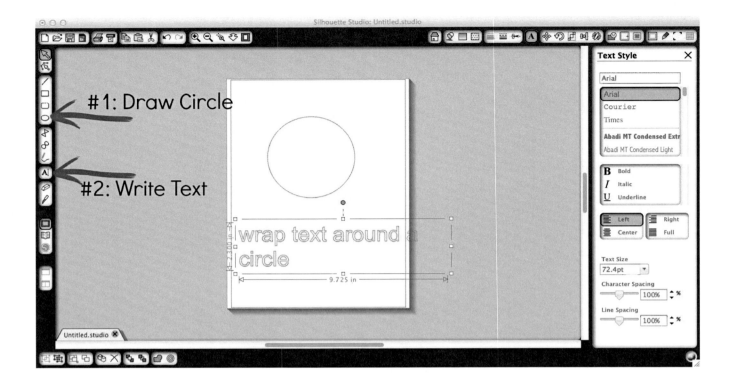

Double click the text so you get the bright green box around it.

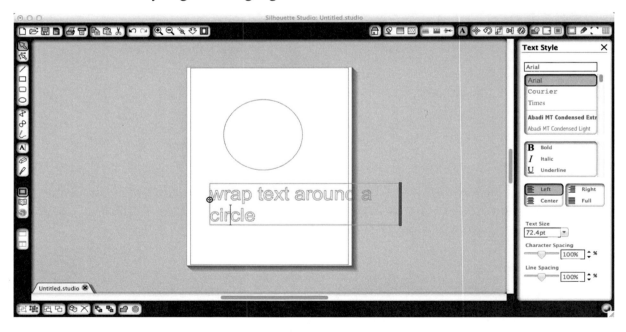

On the left side of the box, a little circle with directional arrows will appear. Grab it and drag it over and drop it right on the border of the circle you drew.

The text will wrap around the circle.

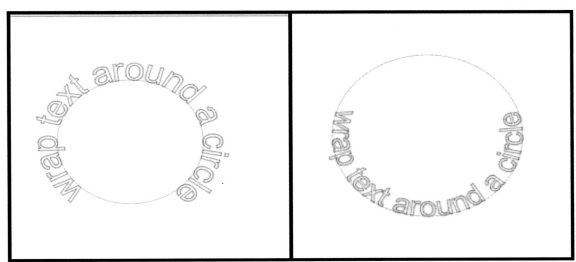

You can move the text to position it exactly where you want it on the circle by dragging that little circle with the arrows around the circle. Drop it on the inside to get the text to wrap around the inside of the circle.

To keep the text curved and remove the circle you must convert it to a path. Do so by Selecting the font > right click > Convert to Path.

Now you can delete the circle or shape and the text will stay in the exact shape.

> **NOTE: Mirroring Curved Text for HTV**
> Converting to path is an essential step if you're designing a text to path design for HTV. If you do not convert to path when you flip the design, the font will become distorted.

Putting Text UNDER a Circle

If you want to put text *under* a circle, you will most likely end up with one of these two below results, which are probably not what you're looking for.

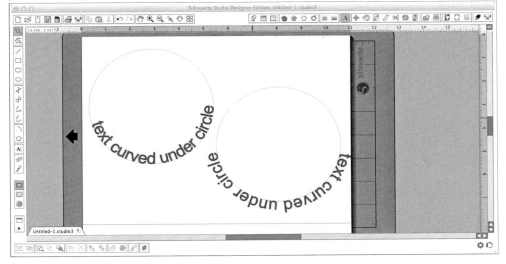

After you've moved the text onto the path, click on the gray oval in the middle of the slider bar and slide it down, towards the outside of the circle. Keep sliding until the curved text moves under the circle.

If the letters are spaced too far apart now, select the text again and use the character spacing slider bar to bring them closer together.

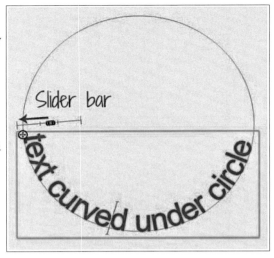

If necessary, grab the circle arrow icon again and move the text so it's centered under the circle.

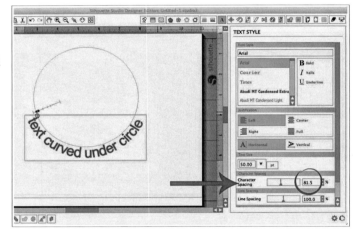

The final step is to right click on the text and select 'Convert to Path'. This allows you to move the text away from the circle while keeping it in the curved shape.

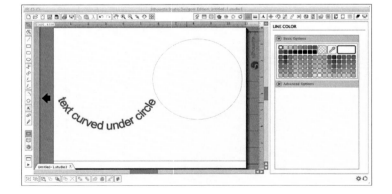

Putting Shapes on a Path

Silhouette Studio only allows for fonts to be put onto a path - not shapes. However, dingbat fonts are a great workaround to put shapes on a path since dingbats use shapes, not characters in the font.

Accessing Glyphs & Special Characters
(for SAMANTHA FONT & Other Fonts)

Samantha font is a Laura Worthington masterpiece. And if you know anything about the Samantha font you probably know that each letter has a lot of aliases....there are dozens of variations of A, for example. However, when you download and install the font (purchase the desktop version) and open in Silhouette Studio only the standard 52 letters are accessed - capital A and lower case a, for example. But you certainly don't want to miss out on all the beautiful Samantha font glyphs and ornaments so you need to access everything.

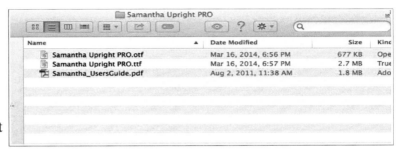

On a MAC you need to be running at least version 10.9 Operating System. Click the little Apple along the top left corner of your computer > select About this Mac and you'll be given the details on what OS you're running. If you're not on 10.9 or greater, you'll need to update to get this easy method to work.

After purchasing, the first thing you want to do is download and install the Samantha font in your font book. With Silhouette Studio closed, Click Download > Access the Zip File > Unzip > Click the TTF file for your Samantha font. (Mine says Upright PRO because that's the version of the font I purchased. Yours may say bold or italics if you purchased those versions.)

Font Book will open > click Install Font. The font will install on your computer.

Open up Silhouette Studio. If you had Studio opened while you were downloading and installing the font, you'll need to close out of Studio and reopen to get Samantha in your Studio font list

Open up Font Book at the same time. Click User to see all the fonts you have downloaded and installed onto your computer. Navigate to Samantha. This is what you'll see right now and you'll probably notice it's missing all the fancy glyphs which is the whole reason you purchased Samantha.

If you go up to the menu bar and click PREVIEW and switch from Sample to Repertoire your view will change and you will have access to the complete font!

The easiest way to open the glyphs in Studio is to copy and paste.

Use the two scroll bars on the right side of the Font Book window to find the glyph or ornament you'd like to use.

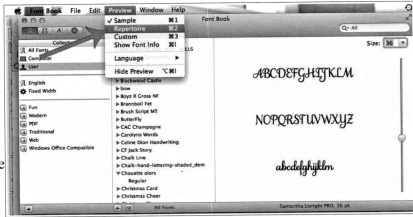

Once you find it, click it to make it blue. Then simply hit COMMAND+C (copy).

**Switch to your Silhouette Studio window and using the Text tool (pp) hit COMMAND+V (paste). The glyph will come into Studio looking like this red box.

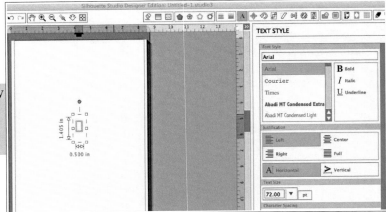

Click on the Text Style Window (b) icon and from the Font Style scroll down to Samantha.

From here click back in the text box. By double clicking you get the cursor and can keep right on typing.

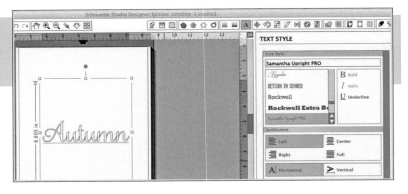

Since your font is still on Samantha the standard Samantha font is used.

Then pick just a *few* letters to stylize - in this case the t and n (you don't want to over-edit your text, do you?).

To change out the "t" and the "n" to the glyphs, go back into your Font Book. Find another letter (t), copy it, delete the current character (t) in the text box and replace it by pasting (t) in the stylized version of the same letter.

Repeat with 'n', etc.

When you're finished editing the font, weld it all together so the letters cut as a solid word and not individual letters.   Select text > right click > Weld. *I've filled it in so you can see just how beautiful Samantha font is.*

And that's how easy it is to use the Samantha font in Silhouette Studio on a MAC.

Windows

To open special font characters and glyphs on Windows you must download the OTF version of fonts that can be opened in the Windows Character Map.

From the Start Menu open up the Character Map.

Once the map opens, check the box for 'Advanced View' towards the bottom left.

From the 'Group By' drop down menu pick "Unicode Subrange" > Private Charchters.

Click on the character you want to use and copy it to your clipboard. Continue from the ** on page 60

Free Commercial Monogram Script Font

Like, Samantha, many of the most desirable fonts that are available for commercial use are fonts that must be purchased.

Of particular interest are monogram fonts. **"Free Monogram"** is a beautiful script font that is not only free, but is also public domain which means it can be used commercially. To use, type the first initial lower case, last initial upper, middle initial lower (ie mVa). It can be downloaded on DaFont.com.

Dingbat Fonts

Dingbat fonts are a great source of designs and what's even better is many of them are FREE!! Dingbat fonts are the fonts that show up as little images instead of actual letters when typed. For example: press an 'A' and a snowflake shows up, hit 'B' and you get a snowman.

Since Silhouette Studio lets users access any font installed on their computer, you basically have access to a whole bunch of *free* designs (personal use only, unless otherwise stated). And because they're fonts, there's no need to manually add cut lines...just like a text font, the lines generated by a dingbat font are cut lines.

A great place to find dingbat fonts is on DaFont.com. Once you find one you like, download and install onto your computer as described in the previous section. Then use the character map (usually found where you downloaded) or just type blindly to add the designs.

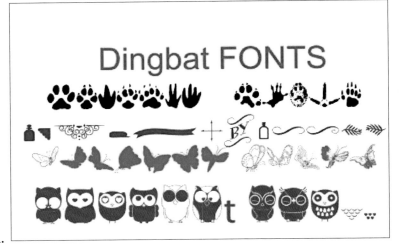

While every image will show up in Studio, not all of them will make good designs for the Silhouette to cut. It's possible to take the original dingbat font images apart so they're even more cut-friendly by releasing the compound path and deleting the parts you don't need in order to make a more cut-friendly design.

In this example, every line of font started with the same characters "Dingbat Fonts". You can see how it changed depending on the dingbat font that was selected.

Saving Designs

Perhaps the most important part of designing is saving the designs and edits to designs. There are several different ways to save .Studio files. All of them are accessed through the File menu along the to menu bar.

Save As... - Save As will save the .Studio file to your computer in whichever folder you direct it to. The next time that .Studio file is opened, it can be edited and the changes will be saved by simply clicking 'Save' (D).

Save to SD Card – Saves the design to an SD card which can be opened directly through the software.

Saving to the Library - Saving to the library puts a design in your Silhouette Studio Library folder called "My Designs" accessed directly through the software program. Changes made to files saved to the library are **not** saved when closed unless the file is saved as a separate library entry with a new title.

Organizing Your Silhouette Library: Keywords & Categories

Saving to the library allows you to add keywords to the design for easy searching and generates a thumbnail image in the library.

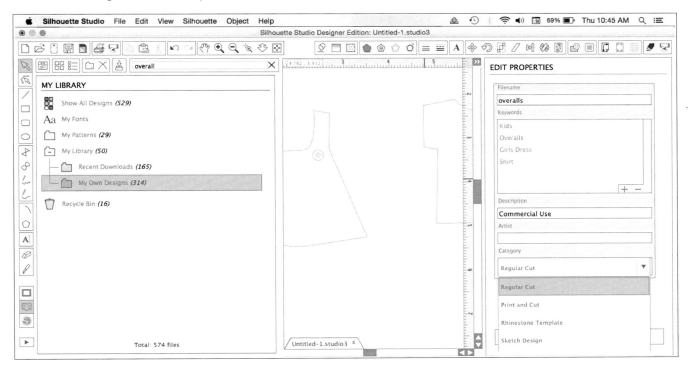

Name the file by typing in a name in the "File Name" box.

Click the +/- to add as many keywords as you'd like.

You can add notes in the description area such as commercial use, personal use only, etc.

To get the most out of organizing your Silhouette Library, take advantage of categories and folders.

To do this, when saving and naming a design click on the Categories dropdown menu. Pick a file type for file: Print and Cut, Rhinestones, Sketch.

To set up folders for each category, go into your Silhouette Studio library. First you need to add a folder for each category, so click "New Folder". Name it Sketch, for example. Add new folders for Print and Cut, Rhinestones, etc.

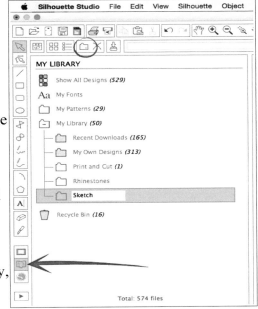

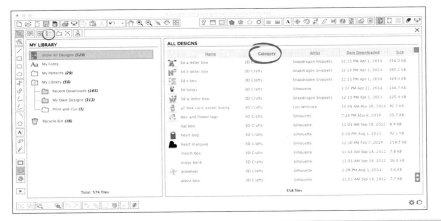

Back along the top, click the icon to "View As a List"

Click on "Category" and the like designs will be sorted by category.

Find the design you want to move into a folder. Click on the design to highlight in blue and then drag and drop it into the appropriate folder.

TIP: Move multiple files, from the same category, into the same folder at once by holding down SHIFT while selecting the file names.

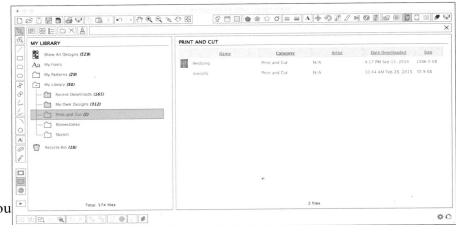

The file will be moved to the folder. When you click on the folder name all the designs you have moved there will be listed. This makes it extremely easy to find certain types of files.

All designs save into the Studio library as "regular cut" unless you pick another category.

To re-assign a design to a new category, right click it > Edit properties.

Click the Categories drop down menu and re-assign the file's category.

Then follow the above steps to pull the file into the correct folder.

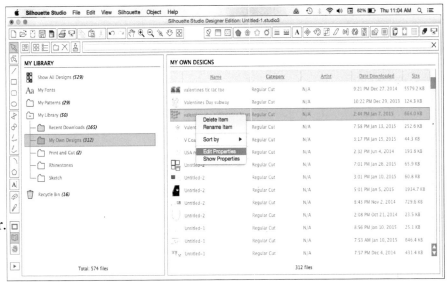

Cutting on Silhouette

Now that you are armed with everything you need to know to work with designs and to design your own shapes in Silhouette Studio, you need to know how to cut them.

The great thing about the Silhouette is that many designs are very versatile so the same design can be cut on paper, vinyl, HTV (with a simple flip), as a stencil or sketch. In this section I'll assume you have mastered designing (or at least become proficient) and will be focused on the next step: cutting!

Things To Know Before You Make Your First Cut

Power on the Silhouette machine, connect the USB from the Silhouette to the computer and open up Silhouette Studio.

Everything that is to be cut needs to be fully inside the cut border on the virtual mat. Turn on the cut border by checking the box at the bottom of the Page Settings window (l).

Moving the Rollers

If you need to adjust the rollers (a feature of the CAMEO only) to cut something smaller than 12" wide, you can do that by first flipping the blue lever on the inside right of the machine. Then pinch the roller firmly with one hand while holding the silver rod with the other. Gently but firmly twist the white roller to unlock the teeth from the rod. You will need to put some effort into this as they don't want to unlock very easily.

> Do not use pliers or any other sort of tool to grip the rollers. You risk marking up the rollers which could leave marks on your materials. Replacement rollers are not available.

After you get the roller unlocked, slide it to the next set of openings so the teeth catch then twist the roller again to lock the teeth into place. Flip the blue lever back down to lock.

Loading the Mat

Load the mat, with the material on it, into the machine by aligning the left edge of the mat with the left most line on the machine. Gently place the mat up against the rollers and click 'Load Mat'. The rollers will start moving and feed the mat slightly into the machine.

PORTRAIT

Load Mat

Mat is fed further into machine

Load Media

Unload

Mat is *not* fed far enough into machine; blade starts cutting too high

Load Mat vs. Load Media

Load Mat is the (default) option you want to select when you are using the mat to cut on. On the CAMEO it's the top option on the digital screen.

Load Media is the selection to use when you are NOT using the mat to cut.

On the Silhouette Portrait, the top gridded button is "Load Mat".

Cutting Without the Mat

It is possible to cut vinyl without the mat. However, only forego the mat if you absolutely have to since you always risk the vinyl slipping or rolling through unevenly.

If you are cutting longer than the 12" mat, I'd suggest investing in a 24" mat. Silhouette America has a 24" CAMEO mat, but not a 24" Portrait mat. However, as a Portrait owner, I have taped two 12" mats together to make my own double-long mat.

Another option is to use the roll feeder. The attachment, which works with the SD, CAMEO and Portrait, holds a roll of vinyl. It takes the weight off the vinyl which prevents it from pulling and slipping. It also keeps it perfectly aligned as it cuts.

If you cut longer than the mat, remember you must tell the software you are doing so otherwise nothing will cut outside the default cut area. To change the Cut Size area, go to the Page Settings window (l). Manually type in the length of your material plus 2 inches or so (just for pad). You will also need to indicate if you are using a 24" mat or no mat. *(You can find more details on cutting longer than the mat or without the mat in the Vinyl section.)*

Selecting Cut Lines

Cut lines are the thick bright red, thick dulled red, or gray lines that are required on a design within Studio in order for the Silhouette to know what to cut. Without cut lines the Silhouette will not cut.

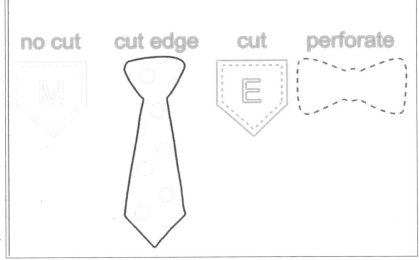

There are several different cut line styles all accessible from the Cut Style window (o).

- **Cut Edge**: Indicated by a Thick Bold Bright Red Line around the edge of a design

- **Cut**: Indicated by a Thick Bold (but slightly dulled) Red Line on the internal lines of a design.

- **Perforate Edge and Perforate**: Indicated by a Thick Dashed Gray Line around the edge of a design.

- **No Cut**: Indicated by a thin red line around the design.

Cut lines are necessary for not only cutting, but also when using the sketch pens. They tell the machine where to cut or sketch. When switched off or to "no cut" they tell the machine where NOT to cut.

Cut lines are only visible when in the Cut Style window.

Select The Material

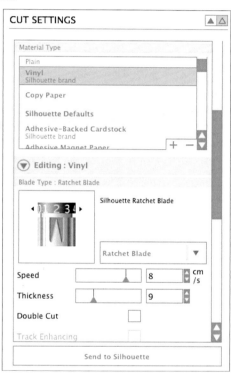

From the Cut Style window (o) you must select the type of material that you are cutting from the long list of default Material Types.

Once a material is selected, another scroll bar will generate allowing you to scroll down further into the window to see the recommended cut settings.

Both the speed and the thickness of the material (determines amount of pressure applied from the blade) will be automatically adjusted by the machine. However, **the blade needs to be adjusted manually by the user.**

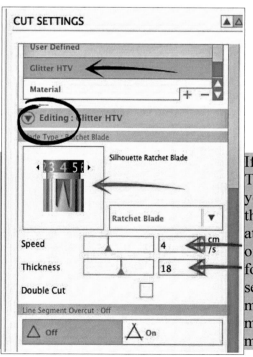

Adding Custom Material & Cut Settings

If you are cutting a material that is NOT listed in the Material Types – such as glitter HTV - you can add your own. However, you will first need to find or figure out the best cut settings for the material. Then to add a custom cut setting, find the +/- signs at the bottom of the Materials List. Click it and type in the name of the material and define the cut settings...customize the settings for everything with a red arrow. All of your custom material cut settings will be saved and can be found at the bottom of the materials list under "User Defined." If you want to delete a material in your User Defined list, simply click on it and hit the minus symbol.

Turning the Blade

The type of material you are cutting will determine the depth of the blade. Use and previously cut materials will also be a factor. (Some materials will dull the blade faster than others; while some will seem to sharpen the blade.) So while the software will recommend a blade depth, keep in mind you may need to tweak it, after a test cut, if your blade is extra sharp or starting to dull.

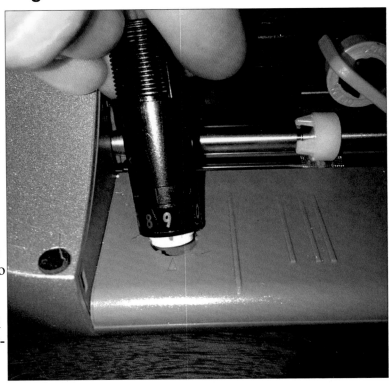

To change the blade depth, remove the blade from the blade holder which is under the cover so that it can be adjusted. On the blade casing, turn the blue lock to the left to unlock it. Slide your blade up and out .

Adjust the blade depth with the ratchet tool that came with the machine or use the built-in ratchet tool to adjust the blade. Put the tip of the blade in and turn to get to the desired number.

Return the blade to the blade enclosure making sure:
- the fin is pointing toward you (6 o'clock)
- the blade is fully down into the holder
- the lock is turned to the right to secure the blade

NOTE: You will need to remove the blade to adjust the blade depth and when you are using sketch pens, a fabric blade, or engraver instead of the ratchet blade to cut.

Recommended Material Cut Settings

Material Type	Blade Depth	Speed	Thickness	Double Cut
Adhesive-backed Card Stock	4	3	29	
Adhesive Kraft Paper	3	3	20	
Adhesive Magnet Paper	6	1	33	
Card Stock	4	3	33	
Cereal Box	7	1	33	
Chipboard	5	1	33	
Clear Printable Sticker Paper	3	4	33	

Chalkboard Vinyl	8	9	3	
Contact Paper (Dollar Store)	2	8	9	
Copy Paper	2	10	15	
Corrugated Paper	8	3	33	
Cover Stock	7	1	33	
Engraving Tool	Pick Sketch Pen	5	33	3x
Felt	10	3	33	2x
Freezer Paper	1	3	2	
Glitter Card Stock	6	3	33	
Glitter HTV	3	4	18	
Holographic HTV	5	8	15	1x
HTV (Flocked)	3	5	33	
HTV (Smooth)	2	8 (slower for smaller designs)	9	(if extremely small)
Leather	10	3	33	2x
Painters Drop Cloth Fabric	6 (Fabric Blade)	5	33	
Patterned/Scrapbook Paper	3	5	30	
Photo Paper	10	15	3	
Printable Canvas Sheet	5	3	3330	
Printable Foil	5	5	33	
Printable Heat Transfer (light)	1	3	2	
Printable Heat Material (Dark)	1	3	8	
Printable Magnet Sheets	4	1	30	
Printer Paper	2	10	15	
Rhinestone Template Material	6	5	33	1x
Sketch Pen	Sketch Pen	10	18	
Stamp Material	9	1	18	
Stencil Material	3	2	33	
Sugar Sheets	4 (New Blade)	2	23	
Temp. Tattoo Paper	4	3	33	
Textured Card Stock	5	3	33	
Thick Fabrics (Canvas/Flannel)	5 (Fabric Blade)	5	33	
Thin Fabrics (Cotton)	3 (Fabric Blade)	5	33	

Vellum	1	6	19	
Vinyl (Adhesive)	2	8	9	
Washi Sheets	1	7	17	
White Sticker Paper	2	8	14	

Test Cut

Perform a test cut from the Cut Style window (o) to ensure that the cut settings work well for the material you are cutting. The test cut takes up about 0.75" square inch of material in the upper left corner of the material. If the test cut is not cutting properly adjust the depth of the blade first. You may also need to slow down the speed at which the machine is cutting to get a cleaner cut.

Cutting

When you're finally ready to commit to the cut, in Studio, click "Send to Silhouette" at the bottom of the Cut Style Window (o) or by clicking the Send to Silhouette icon (p). The blade will begin moving across the page, the rollers begin pulling in the mat and the blade will start humming as it cuts your design.

Is That Sound Normal?

The Silhouette is *not* a quiet machine. However, in most cases the sound that comes from the machine, while cutting, is normal. The official line from Silhouette America is: "Please note that the Silhouette is unfortunately not a whisper quiet unit. The sounds you are hearing are likely normal."

Abnormally loud noise coming from the Silhouette machine could likely be caused by the motor *if* the packing tape that was used to keep it in place during shipping was not properly or completely removed. The manufacturer suggests making sure any tape that was connecting the motor to the side of the machine is completely removed.

When the cut job is complete, the blade will return to the left side and the mat will be spit most of the way out. You will have to push the "Unload Mat" button to get it to fully release from the machine.

Unloading the Mat & Material

To unload the mat and material from the Silhouette, hit "Unload > Enter" on the CAMEO control panel or the Unload Button (third button down) on the front of the Portrait.

It's now time to remove the excess material from around the design. This process is called "Weeding". Some materials are easier to weed than others – such as paper, which is usually as simple as peeling up a corner to expose the cut designs on the mat. Vinyl, HTV, and rhinestone templates will require the use of some tools such as the hook. More details on weeding these designs can be found in their respective sections.

Feeling Overwhelmed by the Capabilities?

One of the most common questions asked by new Silhouette owners is "Where do I start?" It's the question that actually pushed me to write The Ultimate Silhouette Guide, because to be honest there is no stock answer. Because of just how amazing this machine is and how many things it's capable of and able to cut, it would be impossible for me to give every person who asked me the same answer.

Whenever I'm asked this question, as I am several times a week, I always ask "Why did you buy your Silhouette?" Even if you didn't buy your machine, and instead received it as a gift, I encourage Silhouette "newbies" to think about the same basic question. Think about one - just one project you want to create with your Silhouette.

When you think about all the possibilities - the vinyl, paper, htv, stickers, decals, fabric appliqués, print and cut and on and on and on it's easy to see why many Silhouette owners hesitate for months - or years - to take their Silhouette out of the box.

Don't be that crafter who continues to spend hours and hours cutting one 30 piece scrapbook layout out by hand when you have an absolutely amazing machine sitting three feet away that could do it in just a few minutes and with much better precision.

Think about a single project you want to complete. Maybe it's a gift you want to make for a soon to be married couple. Maybe it's a wood family sign or a personalized t-shirt for your granddaughter's first birthday. Or

maybe you are that paper crafter who makes every card and scrapbook layout . Pick one project and focus in on that.

I will lead you by the hand to complete that first project - no matter what it is (because of this, there will be some overlap in each chapter on certain basic design information). As you work to complete your first project you will begin to understand how Silhouette Studio and your machine work and you will be able to apply those same basic skills, tools, and know how to future projects whether they're the same material or something totally different.

Up to this point in the creative process, the designing in Silhouette Studio is basically the same no matter what medium you plan to cut on. But from here on out this eBook is set up like a Choose Your Own Adventure book. You pick what you want to learn and from start to finish we'll get that first project completed.

From there you can pick another "adventure" and learn another skill or concept. Soon you will be feeling more confident in using Silhouette Studio and your Silhouette CAMEO or Portrait.

If you're already comfortable in Silhouette Studio - hurray! But as you know, there's always more to learn about the machine that just keeps on giving. There's always a new trick to learn, workaround to find or troubleshooting tutorial needed. So you, too, pick an adventure and learn something new today about your Silhouette.

Pick Your Own Silhouette Adventure: Materials

Vinyl

Recommended Tools: Scraper, Hook, Transfer Paper

Recommended Retailers: Expressions Vinyl, Amazon for sheets, eBay for rolls

Perhaps even more so than paper, vinyl is a hugely popular material to cut with Silhouette. There are many different kinds of vinyl and there are even more different names for all those different types of vinyl. The most important thing about vinyl is knowing when to use each type.

Deciding on the right type of vinyl for a project, depends on a few different factors including how the vinyl will be used, where it will be placed, and even your personal preferences.

Types of Vinyl

Adhesive Vinyls:

Indoor Vinyl (Oracle 631, removable vinyl, matte vinyl)

Indoor adhesive vinyl is the same as removable is the same as 631 is the same as matte vinyl. They are just different ways of saying the same thing. This type of adhesive vinyl is most often used for vinyl wall decals and indoor signs that won't be exposed to the elements or too much handling.

Outdoor Vinyl (Oracle 651, permanent vinyl, glossy vinyl)

Outdoor adhesive vinyl is the same as permanent vinyl is the same as 651 is the same as glossy. Outdoor vinyl isn't just for outdoors, despite its oft-referred to name. It can be used for pretty much everything besides wall decals. That includes dishes/outdoor projects like mailboxes, outdoor signs, jewelry, wood signs, etc.

Oracal 631 and Oracal 651 are the industry standard and what I would suggest for ease of use, a wide variety of color and size choices.

Heat Transfer Vinyl:

Heat Transfer Vinyl or HTV is vinyl that's applied to clothing and apparel with the use of heat - in the way of an iron or heat press. There is an entire section in this book devoted to Heat Transfer Vinyl so please refer to the next chapter for more on HTV.

Transfer Material:

Transfer tape and transfer paper are essential when working with adhesive vinyl (not necessary for HTV). They are used to move an adhesive vinyl design from the vinyl backing to the surface where it needs to be applied. The transfer material sticks to the front side of the vinyl lifting it off the vinyl backing so it can be applied.

Transfer tape is clear and non gridded and comes in a roll without any type of backing. It's easy to see through which makes applying the vinyl relatively easy.

Transfer paper has more of a sticky paper feel and is gridded to "help" with alignment. Transfer paper has a backing which needs to be removed before the transfer paper can be used to pick up and transfer the vinyl.

In addition, Contact Paper - found in the Dollar Store or other discount stores – can also be used as a method to transfer vinyl designs.

From here on out in this section, when I refer to 'vinyl' it can be assumed I am referring to adhesive vinyl and not HTV.

Before you Make the Cut
Mat vs No Mat

It is true that it is not necessary to use the cutting mat when cutting vinyl. However, I strongly encourage the use of the mat whenever possible. If you cannot use the mat when cutting vinyl because the design, and therefore the vinyl, are too long – consider investing in the Silhouette roll feeder.

Cutting vinyl without the mat requires that the rollers be moved. This is not an easy task. But an even bigger reason to cut with the mat is that it keeps the vinyl in place and from slipping around. When the vinyl slips, which happens far more often when it's not on the mat, the cut will mess up 100% of the time.

Cutting Longer Than the Mat

Silhouette America now makes a 12x24" CAMEO cutting mat for longer pieces. There is not a 24" mat on the market for the Portrait, but if you are in desperate need, as I have been, it is possible to tape two or more mats together to create a long mat.

For very long cuts of vinyl the roll feeder comes in handy because it holds the vinyl in place and aligned. This takes the weight off the vinyl piece which is one of the reasons the vinyl slips or does not cut evenly down the entire piece.

Adjusting the Page Settings

No matter which method you decide to use to cut longer than 12", you must tell the Silhouette Studio you are doing so or the machine will stop cutting at the 12" mark. There are two important steps you must take to cut longer than the mat.

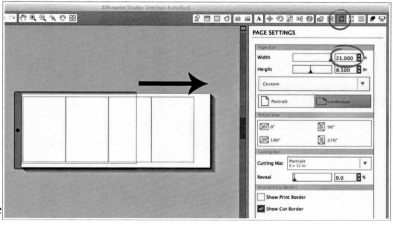

1) In Silhouette Studio, click the Page Settings (l) icon. First adjust the page size. (This is essentially the size of your material aka piece of vinyl).

If your vinyl is 20" long, for example, I suggest you add two or three inches to the length for extra padding - so instead of typing in 20" put 23". Once you do that, you'll see the white area over your mat in Silhouette Studio has extended.

At this point the machine will still only cut 12" long (11" for Portrait users) because by default the cut border is limited by the size of the cutting mat. Can you see in the above image the bottom edge of the cutting mat?

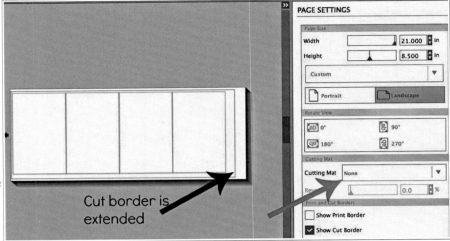

2) The second step you need to take is to change the Cutting Mat preferences. Select the type of mat you are using from the drop down menu.

- 24" mat (CAMEO or two taped together Portrait mats)

- "None" (Roll Feeder, No Mat)

Now you're all set to cut long piece of vinyl.

Adding Weeding Lines to Designs

Weeding lines are an optional – and recommended extra step – that helps cut the vinyl or HTV in the negative space down into smaller, easier-to-manage sections so it's easier to weed. You also don't risk the excess sticking to the actual design while you're trying to weed.

If you decide to add weeding lines, add them last - right before you cut! So do all of your designing, sizing, grouping all that stuff first. Then add your weeding lines.

In your work area, use the Draw a Line tool (ff) to draw a line.

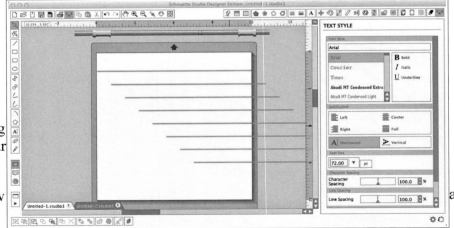

Select the line > copy and paste it.

Repeat until you have about 10 or 12 lines. (The number of lines you need depends on how large your design is. You can adjust to add or delete lines later)

Move the lines so they're about an inch or two apart and all pretty much aligned (they don't have to be exact).

Select all of the lines > right click > make a Compound Path.

NOW open up the design you want to cut. (If the design was already open when you added the weeding lines, select the design and click the Bring to Front tool (x)). You open the design second so the design is "in front" of the lines. It will look like the lines are cutting straight through the design.

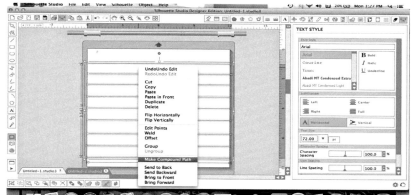

To fix that, select the lines AND the design at the same time and from the Modify window > click "Subtract all."

And now you can see you have added weeding lines in the excess space of the vinyl, but they do not cut through the design.

This makes weeding a breeze!

Cutting and Applying Vinyl

Cutting vinyl with the Silhouette is actually very easy! To get started, pick a simple design that's just a single color...and find something flat to apply it to. Don't try to start with a wine glass or you'll get frustrated. Instead, cut out a simple heart or some other simple shape. Once you get the hang of vinyl - which won't take long - you can move on to more advanced designs and techniques like layering multiple colors of vinyl.

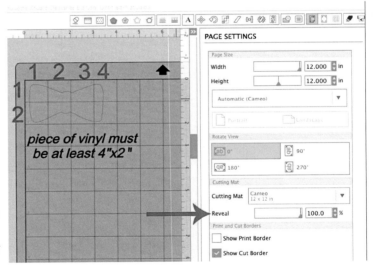

Once you've found your design, open it up in Silhouette Studio and size it if necessary. Place it in the work area in Silhouette Studio. Make any editing decisions and actions now.

From the Page Settings window (o) reveal the grid. This will help you know where to place the vinyl on the mat - and help you know how big the vinyl piece you're cutting on needs to be.

For large and intricate designs, you may want to add weeding lines as described in the previous section.

Place your vinyl on the mat. Be sure the vinyl piece is at least slightly larger than the design and placed in the exact same grid squares as the design in Silhouette Studio. In this example the piece of vinyl must be at least 4" x 2" and must be placed in the top left corner of the mat covering squares 1-4 across and 1-2 down.

The actual vinyl should be facing up with the backing on the mat.

- Load the vinyl and the mat into the Silhouette by pressing "Load Mat" on the control panel of the machine.

- In Silhouette Studio click the Cut Style tool (o) and ensure your design has cut lines (thick red lines) around it where you want it to cut.

- From the material list, click Vinyl and adjust the blade accordingly. The default setting is on a 2, but if you do a test cut and the blade cuts through the backing of the design, put your blade on a 1.

- Click "Send to Silhouette" and the machine will cut the design.

Weeding

When the vinyl design is finished cutting, "unload" the mat and vinyl from the machine. Use the hook tool to carefully "weed" or remove the excess vinyl so only the design is left on the backing. Be sure to remove all of the counters and any vinyl you do not want on your finished project.

Applying Vinyl to a Surface

To move the vinyl design from the backing sheet a transfer material is needed: either transfer paper or transfer tape. Either will work - it's really just a personal preference which you use.

Cut off a piece of transfer tape or transfer paper that's just slightly larger than the vinyl decal. If you are using transfer paper you'll need to remove the sticky gridded sheet from the backing.

Carefully lay the transfer material over the vinyl. Use the scraper tool to burnish over the transfer material and vinyl.

Lift the transfer material up from the corner. The vinyl design should come with it.

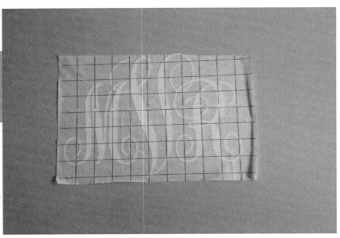

> TIP: Transfer tape can sometimes be 'too' sticky....so blot it on a clean cotton shirt or on your pants to remove some of the 'stick' before applying it to the vinyl.

Now you can place the vinyl design on the surface where you'd like it to go.

Again, use the scraper to burnish over the transfer material and the vinyl. This time when you peel back the transfer material you want it to release from the vinyl leaving the vinyl on the surface as you pull away the transfer paper or tape. It's easiest to pull from a corner in a diagonal direction.

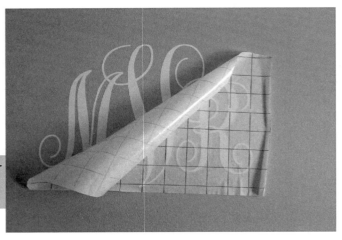

It's also easiest to go slowly and use the scraper tool to keep rubbing your design onto the surface as you pull.

> TIP: Transfer tape can often be re-used so don't throw it away after the first use.

Hinge Method Vinyl Application

The hinge method of applying vinyl or a stencil is a fail-proof way to apply vinyl straight, centered and even.

Cut the vinyl (or stencil), weed, and then apply the transfer paper or transfer tape.

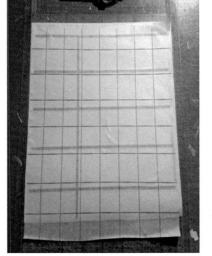

Do not remove the backing of the vinyl after you apply the transfer material. If any transfer paper hangs over the edge trim it so it's the same size as the vinyl backing. This prevents the tape from sticking to the surface making it harder to get the design exactly where you want it.

Working on a flat surface, like a table, lay the vinyl with transfer tape onto the surface where it will be placed. This could be a piece of wood, a canvas, glass, paper, a frame, or in this example, a piece of chalkboard vinyl.

Position the vinyl so it's exactly where you want it and then use a ruler to measure in from the bottom/top and sides to get the design EXACTLY where you want it.

Once you've got the vinyl or stencil straight...put a large strip of painters tape stretching straight across the entire middle of the design. The tape should be taped down to the left side of the table, go over the gridded transfer paper, and then taped

down on the right side of the table.

Remeasure to ensure the design hasn't moved. If it has, lift up one side of the tape and make any slight adjustments.

Grab a pair of scissors and keep them close. Peel back the transfer paper from the top half. Hold it back, while you cut the vinyl **backing** away right along the top of the tape line.

See why this is called the 'hinge' method now? After the backing is removed above the tape, you can place the top half of your vinyl/transfer tape down onto the surface.

Remove the hinge piece of painters tape. You don't need it anymore since the top half is now holding everything in place.

Fold the bottom half up, remove the vinyl backing and then fold the transfer tape and vinyl back down.\|

Use your scraper one more time to rub the vinyl onto the surface and then carefully peel away the transfer paper.

Layering Adhesive Vinyl

Applying Multi-Color Vinyl Designs

Layering vinyl is necessary when working with more than one color of vinyl. The vinyl doesn't literally have to be layered on top of each other to use the method - it just needs to be a design with more than one color vinyl - whether they're touching, overlaid or separate but within the same design.

Open up Silhouette Studio.

Type out your word or bring in the design. For this tutorial, I'm going to be referring to a text design, but know this method will work for layering image designs, too.

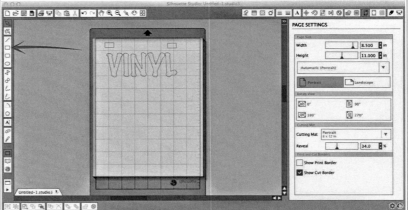

After the text is sized, click the Draw a Rectangle icon (gg). Draw a small rectangle above the top left of your text.

Highlight the Rectangle > Right Click > Duplicate. Move the second rectangle over toward the right side of the design.

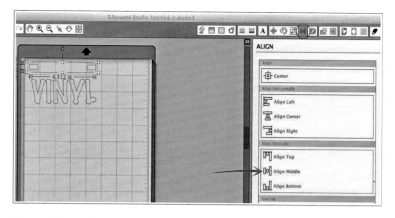

To align the rectangles (sometimes called registration marks) - which are going to act as your layering guides – select them both.

Click on the "Open the Align" Window tool (g) and under the Align Vertically section click "Align Middle." (left)

I wanted to make my design have a big outline so I used an offset.

The offset will be the bottom layer of the design. To get the offset click back on the text > then click the "Offset" icon (Y) > Select "Offset" and adjust the distance to your liking using the up and down arrows or the slider bar > Click apply. (right)

In this example, the offset will act as one layer, the original text will be the second layer.

At this point, the design is all ready to be cut. But since we want to cut on two colors of vinyl and layer them, we need to adjust the cut settings so that only one layer cuts at a time.

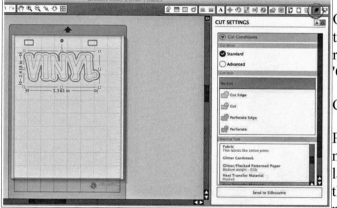

Open the Cut Settings Window (o). Select the two rectangle guides and the offset and set them to 'Cut'. (left)

Click the original text and click "No Cut."

Place the vinyl onto the mat, load the mat into the machine and send it to be cut. Here the bottom layer (the offset) was cut on white vinyl. When the offset is finished cutting, unload it from the machine and set it aside.

Now it's time to cut the top layer...the pink text. It's very important NOT TO MOVE THE DESIGN OR RECTANGLES in Studio at all during this step!

Go back into the Cut Settings window. Switch the cut settings so the offset is now set to "No Cut" and the Text **AND THE RECTANGLES** are set to "Cut." **Since the rectangles are going to be your guides, you want them to cut with both the offset and the text.** (right)

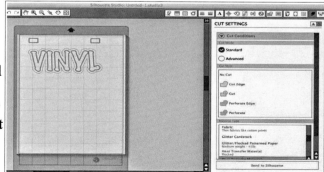

Weed both portions of the design like you normally would. Be sure the rectangles stay in place, too! Here's how the two cuts looked after they were weeded.

To move the top layer (pink) on top of the bottom layer, cut a piece of transfer tape that is large enough to fully cover the largest layer.

Remove the backing of the transfer tape and lay the tape down over the top layer (for me that's the pink vinyl) like you normally would to transfer vinyl to another surface. (1)

Peel the transfer tape/paper up taking the vinyl design with it. Be sure you catch both the rectangles and the design. Don't throw out that piece of vinyl backing just yet! You'll need it.

Place that scrap piece of vinyl backing lightly over the text you just peeled up, but leave the rectangles exposed. (2)

Flip it over so the sticky side of the transfer tape is facing down and line up the rectangles on the top and bottom layers. By putting that piece of paper there you are just making sure the top layer of vinyl and transfer tape don't start sticking to the bottom layer until you are absolutely ready.

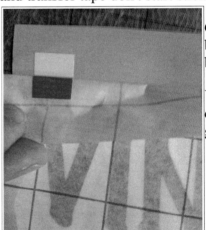

Go ahead and place the top layer rectangles (pink) directly on top of the bottom layer rectangles (white). You may find it easiest to line up the bottom edges of the rectangles and then kind of fold up.

You can't see the white rectangles in the photo below because they are completely covered by the pink top layer rectangles. That's what's going to guarantee you're image is layered exactly right!

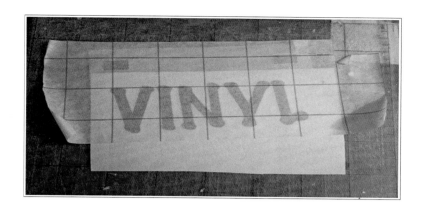

Once the rectangles are perfectly stacked, flip the transfer tape up from the bottom so you can slide out that safety piece of backing or paper (right) then slowly lower down the top layer so it's on top of the bottom layer.

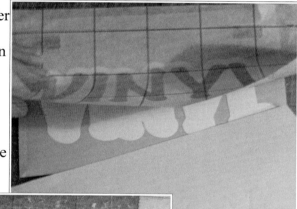

Keep the transfer tape in place and press the two layers together.

Peel the transfer tape up again bringing both layers of the design with it.

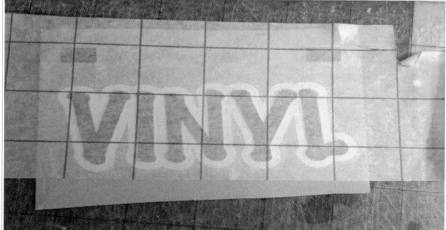

Now you can use the transfer tape to peel up the entire design and place the layered design onto the surface where you want it!

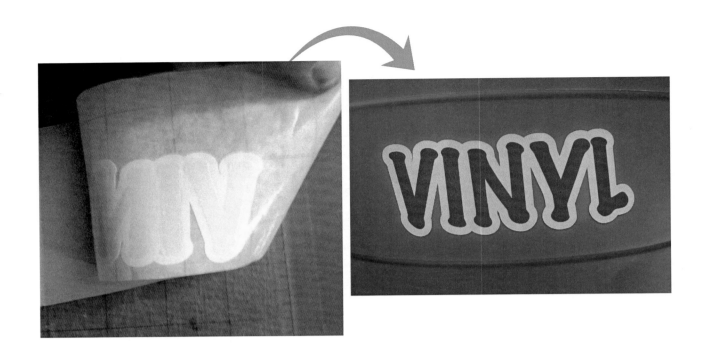

Wet Method Application

The wet method of applying vinyl is a popular one with Silhouette users who will pretty much do anything to avoid bubbles.

The vinyl wet application works on non-porous surfaces where there are no 'pores' in the surface that can trap air or water. For example glass, stainless steel, certain types of plastic, finished wood, painted walls, sealed tiles and porcelain are all non-porous surfaces that are prone to bubbles when vinyl is applied. That makes them the perfect candidates for the wet method because you basically squeegee out the water and the bubbles go with the water.

Cut your vinyl as was described earlier in this section. Have the surface where you want the vinyl applied ready to go.

Fill a spritzer bottle with about half a cup of water. Add a drop of baby shampoo...half a pump will do. If you don't have baby shampoo on hand, liquid dish soap is a good substitute. Mix up the solution in your bottle. Set it aside.

Grab the transfer tape or transfer paper (I prefer the tape since it's see-through and is more 'water proof') and lay it on top of the vinyl design. Do not remove the vinyl from the backing yet.

Use a piece of painters tape to act as a hinge to tape across the top of the design and keep the vinyl in place.

Secure design in place with top hinge or across the middle

Peel back the transfer tape taking the vinyl design with it and then remove the vinyl backing.

Do not fold it down into place yet.

Grab the spritzer bottle and LIGHTLY spray one squirt on the sticky/back side of the vinyl. Do another single-layer squirt on the application surface - in my case it was a piece of glass. You don't want too much of the solution, just enough to mist the area.

Slowly fold down the vinyl design. The solution gives you a little leeway that you can lift back up the design if necessary to reposition. You can also remove the tape if you need to shift the design any. Once the placement is correct, use the Silhouette scraper to burnish the area and at the same time squeegeeing out the water.

Use a clean, dry towel to wipe up the water as you go. Continue to do this - try to go all in the same direction (up and down or side to side but not a combination of both) - until you get as much of the water out as possible.

When the water is all out, peel back the transfer tape leaving the vinyl on the surface.

Wipe up the last bit of water.

Now the design should be on the surface without any bubbles!

If it's a little wet still, just let it sit to dry. This is why it's important to only mist lightly because ideally you get out all of the water as you burnish the layers.

Tips for Applying Vinyl to:

- Wood
  - Paint or Stain Wood
  - Coat wood with polycrylic before applying vinyl to increase the 'tackiness' (optional, but recommended)
  - Use permanent or removable vinyl
  - Do not seal the vinyl once applied
- Tile
  - Get the tile to room temperature before applying vinyl
  - Use permanent or removable vinyl
  - De-stick the transfer tape before applyign to vinyl
- Canvas
  - Use permanent vinyl
  - Spray a light coat of spray adhesive onto the canvas before applying the vinyl
  - De-stick the transfer tape
  - After applying the vinyl/transfer tape, flip the canvas onto a hard surface and burnish from the backside.
  - Peel off the transfer paper from the corner in a diagonal motion
- Glass
  - Clean the glass with rubbing alcohol before applying the vinyl
  - Use permanent vinyl
  - Do not put through the dishwasher; Hand wash only
- Vinyl is not food safe
- Rounded Surfaces (such as wine glasses)
  - Find the largest flat area of the design and make the design small enough to fit in that area
  - Fill the wine glass with water to use as a level baseline to line up the vinyl against**
  - Use clear transfer tape to more easily see the water line
  - Trim the vinyl backing and transfer tape as close to the vinyl design as possible
  - Add vertical slits into the transfer tape to allow you to more easily bend it
  - Place the middle of the design down first then work on placing one side down at a time
  - If you're working with multiple wine glasses and the same design, pour the water into the next wine glass so the design is placed in the same spot.

Heat Transfer Vinyl

Supplies Needed: Scraper, Hook, Iron or Heat Press, Teflon Sheet or Thin Sheet of Cotton

Suggested HTV brand: Siser Easyweed

Suggested Retailers: Amazon; Expressions Vinyl

Suggested Heat Press: Power Heat Press/FancierStudio on Amazon

I highly recommend keeping your first heat transfer vinyl project a simple one, by working with something easy like a t-shirt that has a big open area and is easy to iron or press. You may also want to test out HTV on an inexpensive piece first until you get the hang of it. Many craft stores sell shirts and canvas bags for just a few dollars.

It's also extremely beneficial to have a good quality heat transfer vinyl. Siser Easyweed is the most user-friendly, best quality, easy to weed (hence the name) and economic brand out there. It comes in more than two dozen solid colors and glitter colors.

Designing for HTV

Designing for HTV is slightly different than designing for any other type of medium because the design needs to be mirrored after you have done all of your designing.

So design as you would any other shape/text/design and then mirror. Mirroring or "flipping" can be done by selecting the design and from the Replicate Window (h), clicking Mirror Right.

After you have mirrored the design, you can delete the original.

When the design is ready, prepare to cut it by placing the HTV on the mat with the shiny side down. Load the mat into the machine.

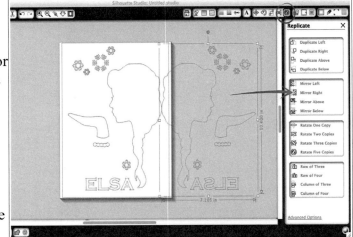

If you are creating a design that has text on a path you will need to be sure to convert the text to a path before mirroring. To do that, pull the text to the path (remember a path can be any shape) > right click > convert to path. If you miss this last step, when you flip your image, the text that's on the path will become distorted.

In Studio go to the Cut Style window (o) and choose Heat Transfer Vinyl smooth (flocked is the fuzzy kind of HTV).

Adjust the blade to a 1 or 2 according to the recommended settings. Perform a test cut.

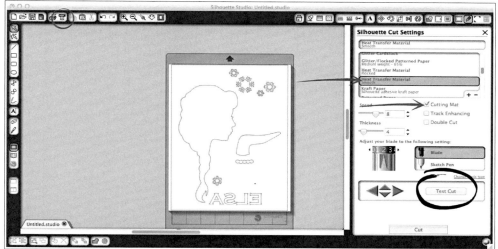

If you have a lot of detailed areas on your design or a lot of small text, slow down the speed and double cut the design so it's easier to weed. You may also want to consider adding weeding lines (see page 74) to very detailed HTV designs.

- Send the design to cut.
- Weed off the excess HTV leaving the design on the sticky backing.
- Heat up your iron or heat press to 305 degrees.

NOTE: You can find the specific temperature recommended to apply the HTV you are using from the manufacturer where you purchased it. Just look for the detailed directions in the item's description.

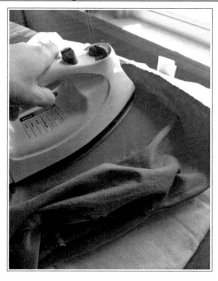

Place the HTV onto the shirt where you want it to be applied. The clear backing should be on the top with the design (now correctly oriented) touching the shirt.

Place a teflon sheet or thin piece of cotton fabric on top and press your iron with a lot of pressure onto the the area. Do not move the iron. Keep it still for about 30 seconds. Then move to another place on the design and press it for another full 30 seconds. Repeat until you've pressed the entire design, an iron-size area at a time, onto the shirt. If you have a heat press, keep the top closed for 20 seconds.

For the Heat Press Method of Applying HTV see page 94

Once the design has been pressed on, carefully peel off the clear plastic backing. Flip the shirt inside out and press again from the inside. This pulls the HTV into the shirt fibers.

Cutting a Multi-Color HTV Design

When you are cutting a multi-color HTV design, I highly suggest you use the fill tool to fill in the color of each piece according to the color HTV you will cut it on. To fill a shape with a color, select it and from the Fill Color Tool (S) pick a color.

If pieces of HTV will be layered on top of each other it's best to actually cut out the shape of the 'top' piece from the bottom piece so that both (or all) are applied directly to the shirt and not actually layered on top of each other, as they will appear. Not only does this method adhere the HTV better to the shirt, it also reduces the bulk and makes the shirt more comfortable to wear.

In Silhouette Studio, move the designs on top of each other, just as you want them to appear on the shirt. It doesn't matter if it's text or shapes or a combination of both. Select both of the designs and from the Modify window click "Subtract All".

Now just select the top layer and pull it away. You can see that you have cut out the overlapping area from the bottom layer.

NOTE: If you resize from here on out, select both the layers and resize at the same time or the overlay won't fit correctly in your cut out!

You could cut like this and try to align the two layers up, but you risk seeing a tiny bit of the shirt peeking through. So to avoid that, make a very small offset around the top layer.

Select the top layer and from the Offset window > Offset > adjust the distance of the offset to .015.

That means a very, very small amount of the top layer will be layered on top of the bottom layer - but just enough that it will prevent any gaps between the HTV and the shirt.

Now you can delete the original top layer and cut the offset.

If you haven't already, mirror both images and then get ready to cut.

If both HTVs are the same type (both smooth, glitter or flock) you can cut them at the same time by placing both of the HTV pieces on the cutting mat in the grid blocks where the designs are on the virtual mat. (See more on cutting multiple shapes as once on Page 96.)

However, if they are not the same, as in this example, where one is smooth and one is glitter, move whichever you are cutting not cutting off of the virtual cutting mat (or turn off the cut lines from the cut style window). Cut the first design.

Then swap the designs and cut the second. Weed and prepare your iron or heat press as described above.

Place the "bottom layer" onto the shirt first. Press it on. Remove the plastic transfer backing. Then place the second/top layer into position and use heat to apply it.

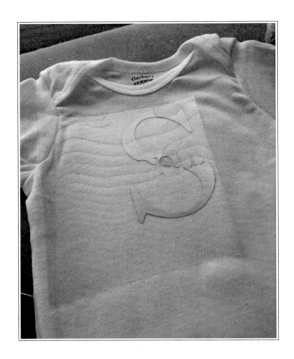 

Remove the carrier sheet.

Flip the shirt inside out and press from the inside.

The 'Burning' Question: Do I need a Heat Press

There's not a stock answer for whether a heat press is necessary, because it all depends on your crafting habits or business. If you are making a onesie here or a bag there for yourself or your family, you probably do not need a heat press - an iron will be fine so long as you get a good seal.

However, if you start getting inquires about making a dozen shirts or decide you want to sell HTV items in your Etsy shop a heat press will take your business to the next level. The stick is better, the time is less, and the effort is minimal.

So is a heat press worth the money for you? Check out this nifty little chart tool to help you decide if a heat press is worth the investment.

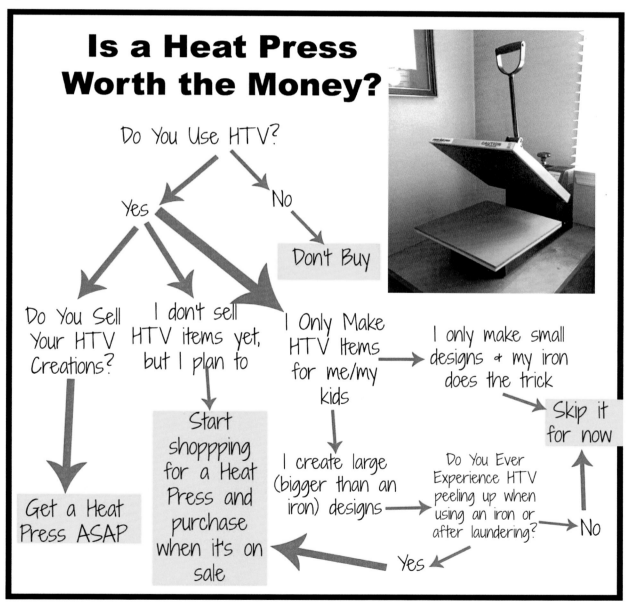

Once you've decided if you need to invest in a heat press, here are a few things to remember:

You want to find the perfect spot for your heat press. A few things to keep in mind:

- Put it on a solid, sturdy surface
- If possible, plug it into it's own outlet
- Keep it out of reach of children
- Don't put it so high that you have to reach up to pull down the top plate
- Have access to the press from three sides
- A ceiling fan (and windows) in the room is recommended because this thing will really warm the room up
- Store the heat press with the plate up/open

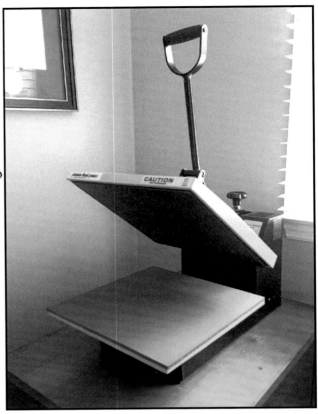

Most heat presses are pretty similar in their operation. There's a power button, a temperature gauge, a timer, and pressure adjuster. Flip on the power button and adjust the temperature using the up and down arrows. If the default on your heat press is different than the recommended time, adjust it too.

You may also want to adjust the pressure knob, although this can be more of a 'get to know your machine' kind of adjustment.

With the top plate up, let the heat press warm up to the necessary temperature while you cut out the HTV on your Silhouette. The machine may or may not beep when it reaches the desired temperature.

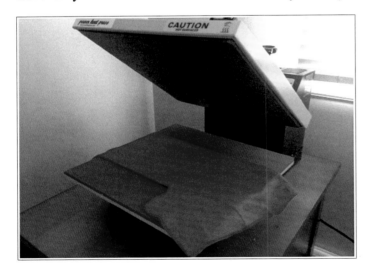

Before you put your HTV onto the shirt you want to pre-heat the shirt. Lay it flat on the bottom plate. If possible, keep the sleeve and neck seams off the bottom plate so you can get better seal. Close the top plate and let it heat up the shirt for a good 10 or 15 seconds. Then open up the top plate and remove the shirt.

To find the middle of the shirt fold the shirt in half length-wise lining up the shoulder seams. Then quickly press down the middle to get a crease exactly in the middle of the shirt.

When you're ready to apply a design to a shirt put the HTV design onto the shirt away from the heat press. Then CAREFULLY lay the shirt flat on the bottom plate of the heat press. Again, try not to have any seams or buttons on the plate.

Before you pull down the handle and top plate, lay the teflon sheet provided with your heat press over the htv and shirt. When you're ready, pull down the top plate locking it down with the handle. On the model I have, the timer starts automatically, counts down and beeps when it's reached the end of the time.

At this point, you can unlock the handle, lift up the top plate, remove the teflon sheet and pull out your shirt.

You should be able to easily remove the clear HTV backing. (Again, check the manufacturer directions - some HTV requires you pull the sheeting off once it's cool.)

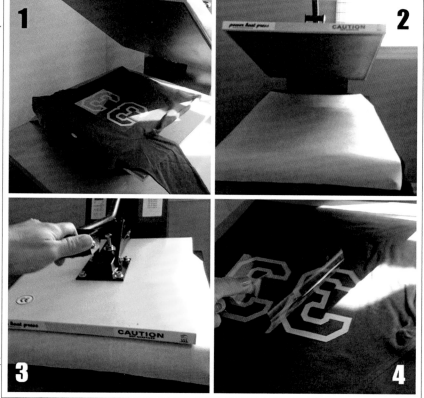

Flip the garment inside out and re-press it with the heat press to draw the HTV further into the fabric.

Paper Cutting

Many scrapbookers and card makers use their Silhouette machines to make beautiful creations and layouts. The detail of the cuts that the machine can make and the huge library of designs and fonts that are available, make the die cut machine an attractive one to paper crafters.

The machine can cut a wide range of papers – everything from contact and freezer paper to card stock and construction paper to chipboard. Designing for and cutting on paper is very straight forward which makes it a great option for beginners or those who just want to test the waters before jumping on in. Paper can be very inexpensive which makes it an attractive place to start experimenting.

Once you've either opened up a design or created one yourself and done all your sizing and editing you'll be ready to cut.

It's a good habit to get into to fill the design with color (or similar pattern) to help with both designing and cutting. This is especially useful if you have a paper piecing project with many different colors. Simply select the design piece and click the Fill Color tool (S) or Fill Pattern tool (U). Then select a color from the palette that's as close to the color or patterned paper you'll be cutting on.

Cutting Multiple Pieces of Different Paper At Once

If you're cutting a card or a scrapbook layout with a bunch of different paper pieces you can cut lots of them at once even if they're different colors – if they're the same type of paper. You don't, however, want to place varying types of mediums together on the same mat, since the cut settings will be different.

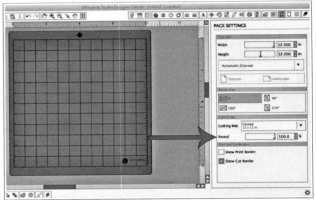

If everything, however, is being cut on the same type of paper – just a different color – you can place it all on the mat at the same time and make one cut.

To do this you'll need to reveal the grid. From the

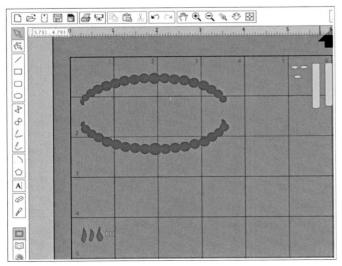

Page Settings Window (l) slide over the bar to reveal the grid. You'll see that the virtual mat has now turned a shade of gray with the grid on it. The grid matches up exactly with the grid on the Silhouette cutting mat.

Move the pieces of the design, grouped by color, into different areas of the virtual mat.

If you've fully revealed the mat, you'll see there are tiny little numbers in each of the boxes along the top and left side of the grid mat. Those also correlate to the numbers on the cutting mat. Use them to figure out exactly where to place the correct color paper on the cutting mat. Place the pieces of paper on the cutting mat ensuring the paper is covering the same grids as the design is in Silhouette Studio.

When you're ready to cut, from the Cut Style (o) menu select the type of cut and the type of paper. The type of paper will determine the cut settings.

A few notes on choosing the correct paper settings:

- Patterned Paper listed in the Material Type is scrapbook paper

- Silhouette brand chipboard is recommended as other chipboards are too thick to fit under the rollers and too thick for the blade to cut through successfully/cleanly.

- Use cereal boxes as a substitute for chipboard

- If your paper is tearing, slow down the speed...a lot.

> NOTE: A very sticky mat can be a nightmare for cutting paper. Either de-stick the cutting mat by blotting it on a clean t-shirt or use a Silhouette brand light stick cutting mat.

Print and Cut

The Print and Cut feature on the Silhouette is perhaps one of the most intimating on the die cut machine. It's also one of the most amazing and powerful. While it's understandable to be a little nervous about your first Print and Cut project, there's no reason to avoid it since it literally will make your crafting and scrapping life easier! Plus, Print and Cut opens up some new options for users – including taking full advantage of the fill tools and creating customized stickers.

I promise you once you do one Silhouette print and cut project, you'll feel more comfortable and confident. Because Printing and Cutting can be intimidating, I'm going to walk you through basics of Print and Cut first and then later in the chapter will touch on customization and more!

The basics can be broken down into four steps:

1) Setting up your Print and Cut file in Silhouette Studio

2) Registration Marks

3) Printing Your File

4) Cutting & Registration Marks

Setting up Your Print and Cut File

First things first: open up Silhouette Studio and pick your design from either the free library or the Silhouette Design Store. The first project you do I would highly recommend using a design that's specifically designed for print and cut (you can search 'print & cut' in the Silhouette Design Store's search box).

Print and Cut designs are indicated with a little "P". There are several free options that come in the Silhouette Library or you can buy one in the Silhouette Online Store.

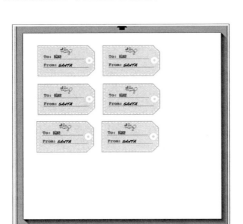

To start, pull your design into the Silhouette Studio work area. I'm going to assume you are using a design specifically designed as a print and cut. We'll get into turning regular cut files and JPEG images into print and cuts later in this section.

Select the design and go to the Cut Style window.

You'll notice there's only one cut line - around the outside of the design. (And in this example, there's also a cut line around the inner circle because it is a tag and the ribbon needs to run through). That's exactly what you want. Everything else will just be printed.

Now you can resize your design or duplicate it if necessary by copying/pasting.

Adding Registration Marks

Now comes one of the most important parts! Click the 'Open the Registration Mark Setting Window' (m). From the 'Style' drop down menu, select Type 1 (for Cameo/Portrait) or Type 2 (SD).

Once you do this a gray area will appear on your work area.

If you are working on a CAMEO go into the Page Settings tool (l) and from the drop down "Page Size" box click "current printer." This will move the registration marks and put a red box (it will not print) indicating the print border.

(Portrait users can skip this step since the machine cuts the same size as a standard printer.)

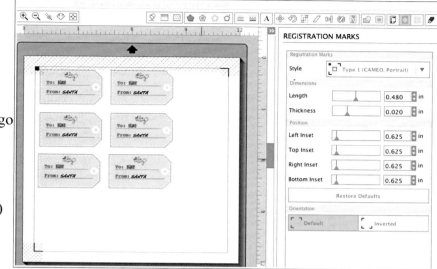

Be sure no part of your design is touching the gray area or the red printer border line. If they are, adjust them so they are inside that space.

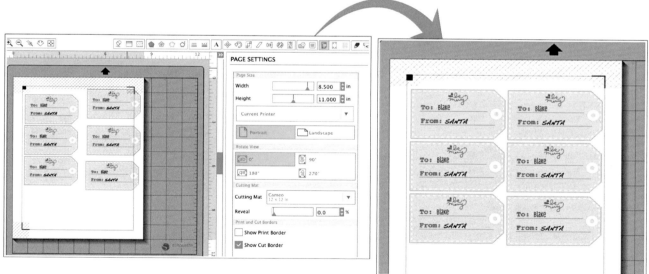

And now we're ready to print...

Printing

Be sure the computer is connected to your regular printer and that you have paper in the paper tray. Then click the 'Send to Printer' (F) button and your design will print.

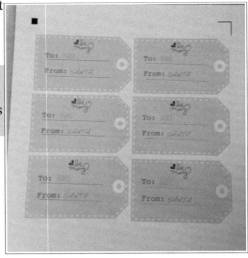

> TIP: Swap the paper out and print on Silhouette printable or clear sticker paper to make your own custom stickers. Just be sure to use the cut settings for sticker paper, instead of paper.

From here on out DO NOT MOVE ANYTHING in Silhouette Studio or the cut will be off.

You can see Silhouette Studio places some markings on the top corners and the bottom left corner. These are registration marks and they are what tells the Silhouette where to cut the design.

Now we're ready for the fun part: Cutting!

Cutting

Take your printed sheet and place it on the cutting mat so the registration marks are oriented exactly the same way they are in Silhouette Studio. Use the arrow on the virtual mat and the top of the cutting mat to ensure everything is correct.

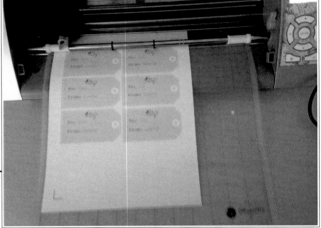

When your mat is prepared, load the mat into the machine and click the 'Send to Silhouette' button in Studio.

At this point, usually the cutting would begin, but for Print and Cut the machine will first use its laser to find the registration marks.

After the registration marks are detected, the machine will begin cutting the design.

When the cut is finished you should be left with your printed design cut out perfectly!

If the Silhouette is having trouble detecting the registration marks see page 137 for Print and Cut Troubleshooting tips.

Color and Pattern Fills

The great thing about Print and Cut is just how customizable it is. You can fill a shape with any color or pattern and print it. Simply draw out a shape – or open one from the library - select it > click Fill Pattern (U) > and pick a pattern.

Silhouette Software comes with dozens of fill patterns – all of which can be scaled to various sizes from the Fill Pattern (U) tool's advanced options.

Patterns can be used to fill not only shapes, but also as prints for custom patterned paper. Just draw a box (gg) covering the entire printable area and print (no registration marks needed).

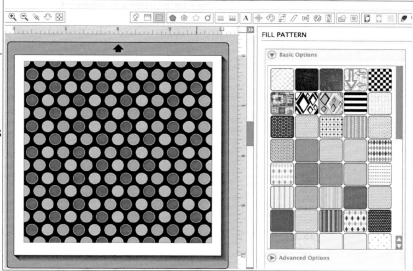

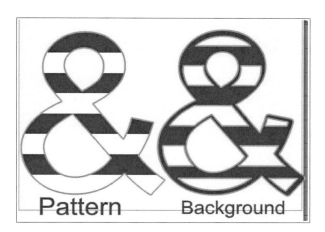

Designer Edition users can add their own patterns by dragging and dropping a JPEG directly into the "My Patterns Folder" in the Studio library. Patterns added by the user will show up in the Fill Pattern window under the basic option patterns and are labeled "My Patterns".

Consider adding photos, logos, and more to your "My Patterns" folder. They work perfectly for Print and Cut and printables designed in Silhouette Studio.

A pattern can also be cut. When the shape of the pattern is actually cut into the design it becomes a 'background.' Quickly and easily turn a pattern into a background by using the trace tool (k).

Turning a JPEG into a Print and Cut

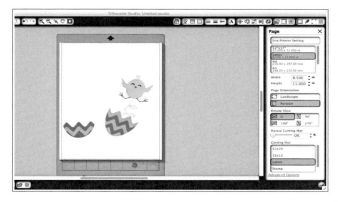

Along with pre-designed Print and Cuts, you can also turn any JPEG, GIF or PNG file into a print and cut file. So if you find a design in an Internet search you can save it as a JPEG or PNG and turn it into a print and cut

Remember - copyright and licensing issues...this is for personal use only unless you have the correct licensing.

101

Once you've found the JPEG image to Print and Cut, save it to the desktop. Import it into Silhouette Studio by dragging and dropping it from the desktop into the work area.

Once the design is in Silhouette Studio, resize it so it fits on the work space. You can do this by selecting the image and dragging in from the corner.

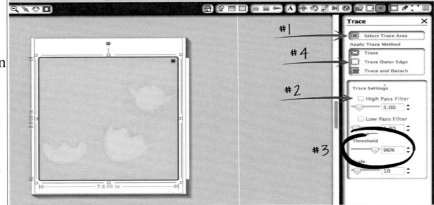

Now use the Trace tool (k) to trace the design (See page 33 for more on tracing). This will create the cut lines.

Click 'Select Trace Area' > Draw a box around the design > ***Uncheck*** High Pass Filter > Slide Threshold Bar Way Up (so entire design is solid yellow) > Trace Outer Edge.

If you were to move the JPEG out of the way, you would see you have a thin red line trace of the image. *If you moved your image too, click undo so the design goes back exactly where it was over the trace. With Print and Cut you want to keep the image and the trace together.*

It's a good idea to group the image and the trace together so they don't get separated or nudged at all or you risk having the cut line off.

Now you can move forward with cutting just like a standard Print and Cut design, which is described earlier in this chapter.

Customizing Print and Cuts

Let's say you purchase a print and cut design from the Silhouette Design Store and you want to change it slightly by maybe adding some new text or changing the color. It's possible to customize Print and Cuts this way in just a few easy steps.

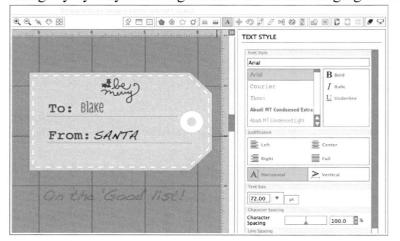

Bring the print and cut design into the Silhouette Studio work area.

To add text to a print and cut design, use the text tool (pp) and type out your text.

To get text or lines to actually show up when printed, you need to either give the line a weight and/or fill the text with color.

Option 1. To keep **text unfilled, but printed**: (This will result in a text outline)
    a. Select the text > click the Line Style tool (a) > adjust the line weight to at least .07. If you want anything other than a solid line, select the type of line you'd like.
    b. Select the text > click the Line Color tool (Z) > pick a color for your line

Option 2. To **Fill With Solid Color**
    a. Select the text > click the Fill Color tool (S) > pick a color
    b. Select the text > click the Line Color tool (Z) > pick a color (to match the fill pick transparent or the exact same color using the color eye dropper)

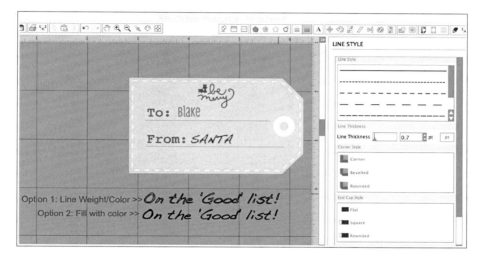

If the text is left as it is now, the Silhouette will treat it as an area that needs to be cut. If you click on the Cut Style window (o) you can see there's a red outline around the text indicating a cut line.

Change the cut style to "no cut" so the text does not cut.

At this point you can stylize the text. Use the text tool to select the font and font size you'd like. When your text is all ready, drag it onto your design and into position.

Highlight the entire design and the text you just added and group them together so they become one design.

When you go to print and cut your design the text will be printed as part of the design, but the Silhouette will know not to cut out the text.

Changing Colors of Purchased Print and Cut Designs

You can also customize the colors of purchased Print and Cut files. So if you purchase a Print and Cut file (marked with a P) from the Silhouette Online Store, you are not stuck with the pre-filled colors. You can change any and all of them.

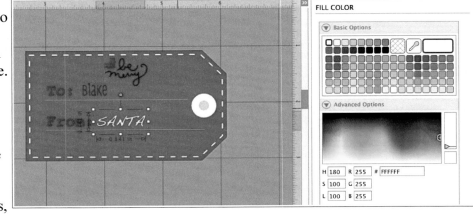

The first thing you want to do is open up Silhouette Studio and navigate to the design in your library or from the store.

Open the design in the work area.

When you select it you'll see it's all grouped together.

To click on individual pieces, you'll need to ungroup...possibly multiple times to access all of the pieces. Now you can select individual pieces and change their colors.

Select your first piece. Then click on the Fill Color tool (S) and click on the new color. If you want to re-color several pieces to the same color, you can select them all at the same time by clicking and holding down shift and selecting all of the objects then pick a color from the fill color tool. The same can also be done using gradient fill (T) or a pattern fill (U).

Move to your next piece and repeat...

Tips for Color Customzing Print and Cuts

- Don't forget to change the line color too!

- If you get to a piece and attempt to fill it, but it fills too much, you need to ungroup more layers and try again.

- You can also fill pieces with gradient options and patterns by selecting those tools instead of the fill tool.

If you have moved the pieces of the design around while filling, put them back into place when you're finished re-coloring and then re-group the entire design.

Before you print and cut be sure you go back in and make sure there is a cut line around the outside of the design *only*.

PixScan

Supplies Needed: PixScan Mat for either Portrait or CAMEO, Latest Version of Silhouette Studio V3

Recommended Retailers: Amazon

Silhouette's Pixscan Technology utilizes a special cutting mat that has pre-printed registration marks on it which allows the user to cut out pre-printed patterns or images. Think of it like you're doing a Print and Cut, but someone else did the printing. It's perfect for double sided print and cuts, cutting out your own drawings, or parts of a design from fabric, scrapbook paper or a card.

To use PixScan you must be using Silhouette Studio Version 3.1.417 or later. Go ahead and download the latest version of Silhouette Studio if you aren't up to date.

Click on the Mac or Windows version to download onto your computer, then you'll need to find the download to install. Just follow the two or three prompts and you'll be good to go.

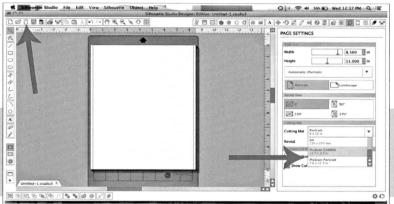

After updating to the latest version of Silhouette Studio, when you open Studio you'll notice a few changes in the software that you did not have in your previous version. There is now a PixScan icon (C) along the upper tool bar and the PixScan mats are listed in the 'Cutting Mat' drop down menu.

The PixScan mat has a cover sheet and a sticky surface just like the regular cutting mats. Make sure you remove the protective sheet before you go any further.

At this point you can grab whatever it is you want to cut and place it on the PixScan mat. The entire material must fit within the black border of the mat. Let's take this detailed card, for example. Any material that you could cut with the Silhouette can be placed on the mat: fabric, patterned vinyl, card stock...

After you have your material on the mat, snap a picture of it with your phone or scan it into your computer. You can take the picture straight on or at a slight angle. However you do it, the entire mat needs to be part of the final image like in the image above. (<< This is the actual photo I used.)

Download the scan or the image (I snapped a photo with my iPhone 5 > emailed it to myself > opened my mail on the computer > downloaded image) to your computer.

Now go back into Silhouette Studio and click on that new PixScan icon along the top tool bar. You'll get a new window along the right side.

Click on 'Import from File' if you downloaded a photo or 'Import From Scanner' if you're scanning.

Then click Import PixScan Image from File.

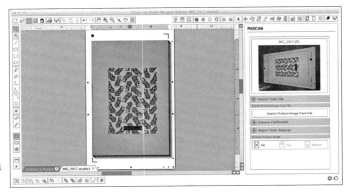

A pop up box will appear. Navigate to the image on your computer and click 'OPEN'.

Your photo will replace the image of that PixScan mat shown in the window as it loads into the software.

Once it's into Studio, the image will pop up in your work area.

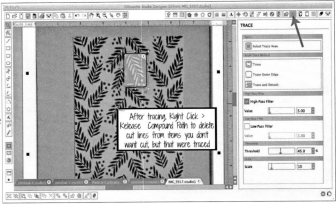

At this point you're going to use the Trace tool (k) to trace the area that you want to cut. I only wanted to cut two of these little branches out. I traced them to get cut lines and then had to release the compound path to delete a few unwanted trace areas (ie. the berries below the branches).

Here's a close up of the two branches that I'm going to cut with the cut lines around them.

Before you send your work to the machine, be sure to go into the Cut Style window and select the material that you're cutting and adjust the blade in your machine.

And now you're ready to cut.

Load the PixScan mat into the Silhouette and click 'Send to Silhouette' in the software.

This side by side of the digitized version and the hard copy really demonstrates just how impressive this PixScan Technology is.

Sketch Pens

Recommended Tools: Sketch Pens, Silhouette Sketch Pen Holders or Amy Chomas Sketch Pen Holder

Recommended Retailers: Amazon, AmyChomas.com

The Silhouette machines can sketch as well as cut. When sketching, the blade is replaced with some type of writing instrument. If you are using the Silhouette brand sketch pens, they will fit into the blade holder without any other attachments. However, if you are sketching with a regular ball point pen, sharpie, marker, or pencil you will need some kind of attachment to keep the pen in place and steady while sketching.

The two main sketch attachments on the market for Silhouette are:

- Silhouette pen holder - comes with three different size pen holders that can be put onto a pen, thin marker or pencil to hold the pen in place while sketching.

- Amy Chomas Pen Holder - A steel attachment that can handle many different size writing instruments thanks to a screw that adjusts to the size of the pen, pencil or marker.

No matter what type of writing instrument you decide to sketch with, the basics of designing a sketch image in Silhouette Studio are the same as designing a shape or text to be cut.

Start with a simple – single color – sketch design. Set up the design the same way you would a cut file. Just keep in mind instead of the machine cutting the design along the cut lines, it will draw the cut lines.

It's important to remember, the design or font will not be "filled" in unless you take extra steps to ensure that it is. See page 113

When it comes time to cut, from the Cut Style window's material list select "Silhouette Sketch Pen". Then you'll get another scroll bar, scroll down to the 'Editing' menu where you can select the sketch pen rather than the blade.

Load the paper onto the cutting mat and into the machine.

On the machine, remove the blade and replace it with the sketch pen or sketch pen and attachment depending on what type of pen you are using to sketch.

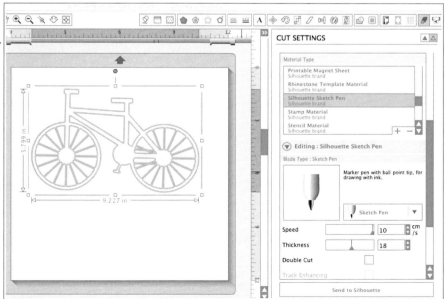

TIP: To prevent stray lines being drawn across the paper, ensure the writing instrument is the proper distance from the paper. Place a popsicle stick between the tip of the pen and the paper. When the tip of the pen hits the popsicle stick, it is at the perfect distance from the paper.

Lock the pen and/or attachment into place and remove the popsicle stick. Doing this ensures the pen is at the right height and will not drag across the paper leaving stray marks.

Now you're ready to cut so hit "Send to Silhouette" in the software and the pen will start sketching on the paper.

Cutting Out Sketch Pen Designs

If you'd like to cut out a sketched design...go through the entire process described above, to sketch the design onto paper. After the design is sketched, however, <u>do not remove the paper or the mat from the machine.</u>

It's also important NOT to move your design around the Studio work area at all. Any little nudge will cause the cut to be off.

While the mat and paper are just hanging out, go back into Studio to make some adjustments.

Select the entire design.

Go to the Cut Style Window > Click Cut Edge.

If you go to the Cut Style window and click "Cut Edge" and more than just the outer edge gets a cut line it's due to a compound path. A compound path makes all those white spaces "hollow" so in essence everything would be an edge.

To get the cut line around the outer edge of the design only, release the compound path. Right Click > Release Compound Path. Now re-highlight the design and click 'cut edge' again to get the cut line just around the outside edge only

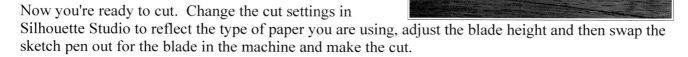

If you leave it to cut like this the cut will be made exactly on the outside sketch line - which may be what you prefer. If so, skip this next step and pick up where you see the * below.

OPTIONAL: If you prefer to have a little tiny gap between the sketch line and the cut line so none of the sketch lines are cut you need to add an offset. To do this, highlight and click the 'Open the Offset Tool' button. Click 'Offset' and adjust the distance of the offset. Click apply. Now highlight the offset you just created and from the Cut Style window select it as 'cut edge'. Select the rest of the design and click "No cut"

Now you're ready to cut. Change the cut settings in Silhouette Studio to reflect the type of paper you are using, adjust the blade height and then swap the sketch pen out for the blade in the machine and make the cut.

If you haven't moved the design in Studio OR the mat out of the machine you should get a perfectly lined up cut since the machine basically believes it's making the same cut again - only this time it's doing it with the blade instead of the pen.

Sketching a Multi-Color Design

To sketch a design with more than one color sketch pen, it's just a matter of a few clicks and pen swaps.

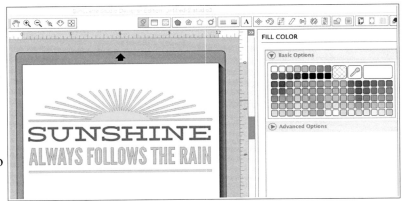

Open up the design in Silhouette Studio. If it's all grouped together or is a compound path, you want to release and/or ungroup the design so each piece can be selected separately. This is necessary because you need to be able to assign each piece a color and cut style.

Once everything is completely ungrouped click on the individual pieces and use the fill tool to fill them in with the color sketch pen you want to sketch them with. *This does not actually tell the machine what color to cut, it's just a reminder to you of what color pen you should be using and when.*

Group all of the same color pieces together. If need be, re-make the compound paths.

Now it's time to assign each part of the design a time to cut. Pick one color to start with and select all of those pieces. Go to the 'Cut Style' Tool and click "Cut" and from the materials list "Sketch Pens."

Select all other colored pieces in the design and pick "no cut". (You can easily tell they will not cut because there is no bold red cut line around them).

Swap out your blade and put in the first pen or marker. Send the first color to cut/sketch.

TIP: When the first part of the sketch is finished, DO NOT REMOVE the paper or mat from the machine when it's finished cutting and do not move any part of the design in Silhouette Studio.

Go back into Studio and select the part of the design that just sketched and from the cut style window change the cut style to "No Cut".

Then select the second set of designs to sketch and from the cut style window select 'Cut'. Swap out the sketch pens in the Silhouette and send the design to sketch.

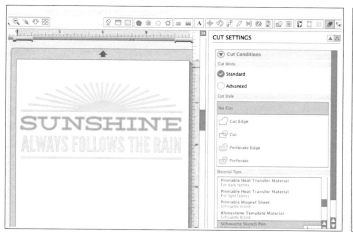 

Again, do not remove the paper or mat from the machine.

Repeat the process of swapping the pens and turning on/off the cut lines until every part of your design has been sketched.

Only when you have finished sketching the entire design can you finally remove the paper and mat from the machine.

Filling in Fonts with Sketch Pens

As was briefly referred to at the beginning of this section, the sketch pens will only draw the same way the blade will cut - an outline. But if you are not looking for an outline and would like your design filled in you need to make a few adjustments to your design. The key is the offset tool.

Start by typing out the text using the Text tool (pp). Pick the font size now because after you do the next step you won't be able to adjust the actual font size. You will only be able to resize by dragging the corners in and out.

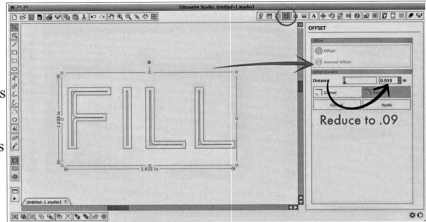

After the font is sized and the style is selected, zoom in really, really close using the Zoom tool (N). Closer!

With your font selected, click the 'Offset' tool (Y) button, then select 'internal offset.' You'll see the offset appear inside the letters.

If the internal offset is a little too far away from the original outline, which it likely is, you need to reduce the distance, so drop that value down a bit.

Adjust the distance, using the up and down arrows so the internal line is very close to the original font outline. A good starting inset is a .09" distance. Click apply.

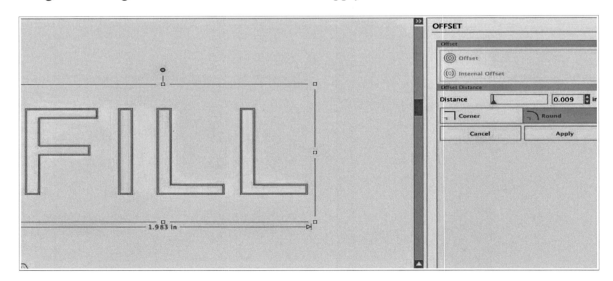

It may be tough to see that there are two lines there...but that's what you want. You want them very close together so that when you repeat this over and over again it 'fills' in the font.

Repeat this same process again with an inset at a slightly further distance. For instance, the second inset may be at .19; the third at .29 and so on. Be sure to click apply after every inset. After a few insets, you'll see how your font is starting to fill.

Repeat the internal offset as many times as needed until all the letters appear to be filled in.

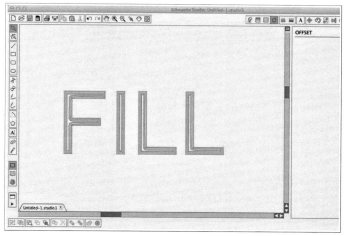

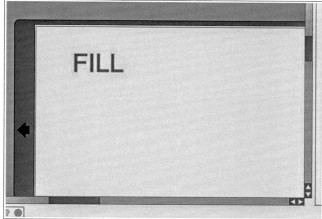

With every internal offset you generate, you are creating a new sketch line. All those sketch lines closer together give the illusion that the font is filled.

The size of the font and the distance of the internal offsets will determine exactly how many times you need to create the offset. Now remember you are zoomed in really close so you can see the tiny gaps between the lines. When you zoom out (O) - it will be almost impossible to see that there is any space between the insets.

Before you move or resize the text, be sure to select the entire design and group (q) it so all the insets stay together. When you send it to sketch on the Silhouette the font will appear to be filled in.

Filling in Designs with Sketch Pens

Just like with fonts, you may want a sketched designed filled in. However, unlike filling in fonts, Designer Edition is necessary to fill in designs.

To start, open the design in Silhouette Studio. *Note: This same method will work with* photos traced using this process.

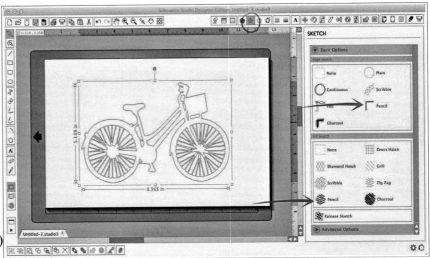

As the design is now, the only cut or sketch lines are the red lines you see which will result in an outline of the design.

To fill in the design, select it and open up the Sketch Tool window by clicking on the Sketch Tool icon (W) along the top. Again, you need DE to do this otherwise you will not have this icon.

For the Edge option select your choice. In this example, I went with 'pencil' because I sketched my design in pencil and I wanted it to look the most authentic.

For the Fill Sketch option select your choice. Again, I picked pencil. This is the result I got after my initial two selections. It's okay but it's certainly not 'filled.'

Now click the down arrow to open up the Advanced options. This is where you'll really tell the software exactly how to fill in the design.

You'll get more edge and fill options. There are a lot...and I mean *a lot*...of areas to fill in the bike. So I need my sketch lines to be pretty dense and spaced pretty close together to get the full fill effect I'm looking for.

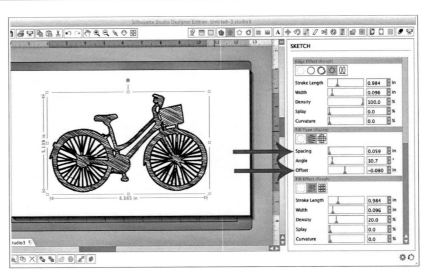

In the window where you have all of the slider bars start with Spacing. I reduced the spacing as far down as possible (to the left) to about 0.059 so the zigzags were very tight producing more of a colored in look.

I also adjusted the offset to -.080. With those two changes I went from the image on the previous page to this...

If you feel the need, tweak the remaining slider bars as you see fit. I like to slide them just slightly one way and then the other to see what it does to the design. You can always click "undo" to undo your previous edit.

TIP: Reduce the 'splay' slightly to reduce how much you've colored outside the lines.

When you are happy with your filled in sketch design you can get ready to send it to your Silhouette to sketch.

This sketching process is NOT a fast process. It will make your software, machine, and computer work hard. You will get the 'generating cut' and processing cut status bars and wonder if they will ever complete. You may even be tempted to hard close the program thinking there's an error. Don't. Just be patient. It will move on to sketch...it just takes time. Remember, each of those tiny sketches is a 'cut'.

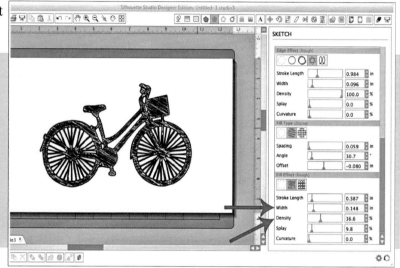

Stencils

The Silhouette is great for cutting stencils for all kinds of projects including painting, fabric paint, and etching. Stencils can be cut on a variety of materials including Silhouette Stencil Material, vinyl, contact paper, and contact paper – all depending on where the stencil will be placed. Silhouette Stencil Material is re-usable while the other three options listed are one-time use stencils.

In Silhouette Studio, design a stencil just like you would any vinyl design as described in the vinyl section.

The easiest way to ensure the stencil fits on the surface is to make a mock up. Start by first measuring the surface where the stencil will be placed.

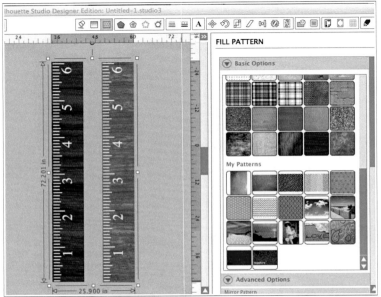

In Studio, use the Draw a Box tool to draw out a box the same dimensions as the surface. For example, if the surface is 60"x10" draw out a box > click the 'Scale' icon to manually type 60"x10". A box that size, for a growth chart will obviously be much larger than the work space, so zoom way out (O) so you can fully see the design.

Fill the box with the same color that you plan to paint the surface. You can even fill with a wood-grain pattern if your surface is stained.

Open up the design that will be used for the stencil or type it out if it's text. Fill in the text or design with the same color you plan to paint it.

Drag the stencil design on top of the box/wood and position and size it so it fits nicely on the surface. Remember, the mockup surface is the same size as your actual surface, so sizing the design this way will ensure it fits after you cut it.

If the stencil has text, keep in mind that unless you are using some kind of transfer material to move the stencil onto the surface, it will have to be hand placed, including the counters. You can get around this by using a stencil-friendly font such as "Stencil".

The other option is to slightly alter the font to make it more stencil-friendly.

Manipulating Fonts to Make Better Stencils

The middle part of letters like a, b, d, and g is called a 'counter.' When you cut a stencil that includes letters with counters you have to hand-place the counters so that the letters are formed properly in the stencil. OR you could slightly modify those letters to avoid the counters.

This slight tweak makes the letters all one cut and will eliminate the counter altogether so there's no positioning, losing small pieces, or gluing your fingers together trying to slide the inner 'e' into place. It's some work up front, but it will save you the headache later - especially if you save the modified font files you create.

First things first - you must pick a good starting font such as Great Vibes. It has *some* letters that already avoid the counter and some that just need to be slightly modified. It's also a good basic script font and using it in Silhouette is nice because the letters can easily be welded together. A font like this is great because a few letters (a, b, q) with counters are already designed to avoid that extra weeding since they have a little space that breaks up what otherwise would be a counter.

My suggestion is to:

1) Pick a font you use often to modify

2) Save the .studio files created with the new fonts so you have them for future reference.

Type out your letters > ungroup and zoom in.

I'm going to focus on 'd', but the process is the same for all the letters (script or serif/sans serif).

As you can see the 'd' connects at top of the rounded area and the vertical. (The b does not, coincidentally.) Inside that area is where we get the counter. To eliminate that round space, you need to break up that middle area. To do this, use a combination of both the Knife (rr) and Edit Point tools (ee)

Start by zooming in really close to that intersection. Use the Knife tool to draw a slice in the area of the intersection. (left most image)

That's a tiny slice. It needs to be slightly bigger so the medium doesn't tear when it's cut or when weeding.

> NOTE: If you have Designer Edition, you can also use the eraser tool and set it to 'solid' to avoid the next few steps.

Make a second slice just slightly to the left. This makes a little rectangle-ish piece. (middle image)

Select the piece and delete it. (right image)

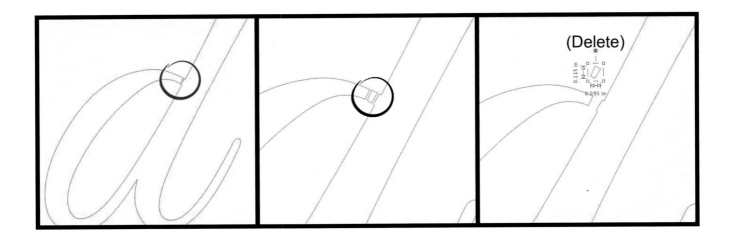

(Delete)

At this point you can see that when the Silhouette cuts the 'd' there will be no need to weed the counter because it's sort of built into the letter already.

However, you may want to smooth out the area so click on your edit points tool (circled) > double click the design and move the edit points around or delete them until the lines are smooth.

Some letters may be trickier than others, but just get creative on where you're making the cuts and you'll soon eliminate all those counters!

I highly suggest you save the letters you have modified to your library so that you don't have to recreate them everytime you want to use them.

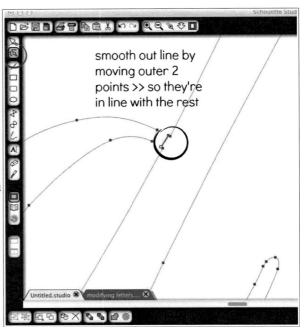

smooth out line by moving outer 2 points >> so they're in line with the rest

Cutting Stencils: Picking the Right Material

When you are ready to cut the stencil consider the surface where the stencil will be placed to determine the best cutting material.

- **Adhesive Stencil Material:** Best for stencils that need to be used more than once
- **Vinyl**: Works well on wood (consider the PVPP method) and glass
- **Contact Paper**: Cheaper than vinyl but not as sticky; will work on wood and great for glass etching (more in the next chapter)
- **Freezer Paper:** Works well when ironed onto burlap and other types of fabric; cannot be used with transfer paper

Cut the stencil using the recommended cut settings in Silhouette Studio. If you are working with contact paper or freezer paper, refer to the cut settings listed on page 68.

Most stencils will be "reverse weeded" which means the cut design will be removed, so it can be painted, and the negative space will be left intact. Typically, the negative space is removed during weeding so that the design can be transferred.

The only time the negative space of the vinyl (or other stencil material) is removed for a stencil is when using the PVPP method.

PVPP: Paint Vinyl Paint Peel

For PVPP (Paint Vinyl Paint Peel) the surface is "**P**"ainted a base color. That base color will be the color of the design when it's all finished.

The "**V**"inyl is transferred onto the surface like it normally would be using transfer tape or transfer paper.

A second coat of **"P"**aint, in a different color, is then painted over the entire surface and the vinyl.

> TIP: To prevent paint bleed, paint the edge of the design/stencil with a small amount of either the base color paint or mod podge. This will seal the stencil down and anything that bleeds under the stencil will either be the same color as the base coat or clear.

Finally, the vinyl stencil is "**P**"eeled up. In the areas that the stencil covered, the base coat will show.

Freezer Paper Stencils

Freezer Paper stencils can be cut and then hand-moved onto any surface where they can be ironed. Place the freezer paper stencil down onto the material with the shiny side down.

Temporarily adhere the freezer paper to the fabric with an iron. The freezer paper gives a good seal when ironed well.

To paint, avoid using too much paint and blot the paint on in an up and down motion rather than strokes to avoid getting paint under the stencil.

Stencil Material, Contact Paper and Vinyl Stencils

For wood projects, vinyl and contact paper stencils work well because the material is both inexpensive and adhesive.

- Paint or stain the surface of the wood first.
- Use transfer paper to move a vinyl or contact paper stencil into place on the surface. (It should have been reverse weeded).
- Seal the edges of the stencil with mod podge to prevent paint from leaking.

- Paint the stencil and then remove the stencil.

TIP: Seal stencil edges with mod podge before painting for crisper lines!

120

Etching

Supplies Needed: Glass surface, Stencil material (can be vinyl, Silhouette stencil material, or contact paper), Etching Cream (I prefer Armor Etch), Painter's Tape, Paint Brush, Latex Gloves, Water

Recommended Retailers: Dollar Store for glasses, contact paper; Amazon or craft store with coupon for for etching cream

Many people like the look of etched glass because it's timeless and classy. It's also able to go through the dishwasher, unlike vinyl designs placed on glassware. Etching is actually a very easy and fast process.

Open up Silhouette Studio and create or open up your design. For your first etching project, it's best to use a design that's not too detailed.

The size of the stencil will be determined by the glass surface. If you're working on a rounded surface, like a mug or glass, it's best to size the stencil so it fits on the flattest part of the rounded surface. If you make your stencil too big it will gap and you will have etching cream bleeding under the stencil.

You can cut the stencil on either the Silhouette Stencil Vinyl, adhesive vinyl, or contact paper. Follow through the Stencil section to cut your stencil.

Before applying the stencil, clean the glass by wiping it down with rubbing alcohol so it's free of finger prints and smudges. Dry the surface really well.

Once the stencil is on the glass surface securely, tape off the edges with some painters tape. This will prevent any of the etching cream from getting on parts of the glass where you don't want it.

Before you start etching...gather all of your supplies. The etching process is really fast and you want to make sure you have everything handy because leaving the etching cream on too long could mess up the end result. Set up near a sink and protect your surface.

Etching Cream is pretty powerful stuff…so, don't skip the gloves.

Open up the etching cream and using the paint brush, blot a thick layer across the stencil. You want it thick so don't be afraid to really gob it on there. Try to make the layer of etching cream as even as possible across the design.

Set the timer and wait.

The manufacturer recommends leaving the etching cream on the glass for 1 minute, but I find I get a better result when the etching cream sits on the surface for at least 4 minutes.

When the time is up, run the glass under luke warm water to remove the etching cream. Once all the cream is off, remove the stencil. I like to let it sit for a few minutes before rewashing and drying the glass.

Rhinestones

Cutting rhinestone designs with your Silhouette can give your project or apparel a little extra bling. You do not need to have Designer Edition to cut rhinestone designs, but you do need to have DE to create your own custom rhinestone designs.

A few Golden Rules of Rhinestones:

* Never resize a rhinestone design
* Be sure to have the correct size rhinestones
* Cut rhinestone templates can be reused over and over again
* Bring your patience

When purchasing a Rhinestone design the circles are exactly the size of the rhinestones so *you can NOT resize the design* or the circles will change sizes along with the design and your rhinestones will not fit correctly!

You also want to make sure you're purchasing the correct size rhinestones to fit the template. Silhouette cuts 6ss, 10ss, 16ss, and 20ss size rhinestones.

The best value is to either get the Silhouette Rhinestone Starter kit or the Template Kit plus at least one package of rhinestone for your first rhinestone project. After that you can purchase packs of rhinestones, in various sizes and colors.

To start, open up Silhouette Studio...then open up your design.

Again you won't be able to create your own rhinestone designs unless you have Designer Edition, but you can purchase a Rhinestone design from the online store.

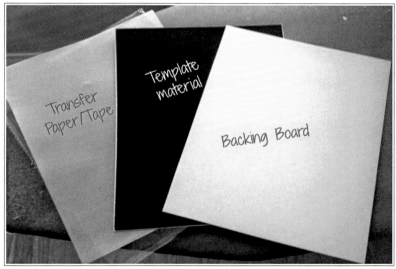

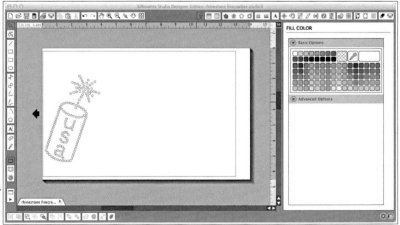

Again, DO NOT RESIZE THE DESIGN!!! Resizing will stretch the circles which are each a place holder for a rhinestone and they are sized exactly.

As you prepare to cut, move the design to the side and the corner of the virtual mat so it's not wasting your template material by cutting in the middle. That way you can make more rhinestone templates out of the same sheet.

You will be cutting on the black fuzzy template material so load your template material onto your mat and from the Cut Style window in Silhouette Studio pick 'Rhinestone Template Material.'

You'll have to increase the blade depth to a 6 or 7. Just follow the recommended cut settings provided in the software. Perform a test cut before sending the full design to cut.

When it's finished cutting, you'll probably have trouble seeing the actual circle cuts through the black fuzz. But if you flip over the template material, you'll be able to see them easier to make sure they're actually there. Cut the design apart from the rest of the template material sheet so you can reuse that piece.

Remove the white backing. The best way I can describe this is to pull the black piece off quickly as if you were quickly removing a band-aid. The faster you peel off the black template material, the more little black dots will be left behind.

If some circles come up with the template, use the hook tool to pop them out or flip the white backing piece over, laying the sticky side of the black template material down on it and rip it up again to try to get those dots to stick.

Lay the template material onto the thick white backing board. Again, do this in the corner, not right in the middle, so you don't waste space and materials. *You can actually use that white space to add more rhinestone templates for future projects.*

If you are only working with one color of rhinestones, you can dump a small pile on top and use a brush or the Pick Me Up tool to work them into place.

TIP: If you are working with several different color rhinestones, use a piece of transfer tape to cover the holes that should NOT be filled before adding the first color rhinestones.

Use a small brush or foam paint brush to nudge the rhinestones into place. Use the hook tool to flip over any upside down rhinestones.

124

When all the holes are filled with rhinestones, take the white backing off the clear sticky transfer sheet and carefully place it on top of the rhinestones. Press the transfer sheet down directly from above, covering the entire design at once. If you try to start at one end and then 'roll' your way to the other end some of the rhinestones will shift out of place. Press down gently so all the rhinestones stick. If any are out of place use your finger nail through the transfer tape to try to 'snap' them back into position.

Once they're all stuck on there really well, peel the transfer tape up bringing with it ALL the rhinestones. Now you can move the entire design to your shirt and from here on out it's like applying HTV.

Leave the transfer sheet/tape in place, put a thin cotton fabric piece over top, and use your iron or heat press to press down. The iron should be on the 'Wool' setting with no steam. You want to press for about 15-20 seconds to get the adhesive on the back of each of those tiny rhinestones to melt into the fabric.

Once the rhinestones are set into the fabric, you can pull off the transfer sheet.

The last step is to flip the piece of clothing inside out and re-iron the rhinestones from the back of the design.

Creating Custom Rhinestone Designs

To create custom rhinestone designs you will need to have Silhouette Studio Designer Edition. The one-time paid upgrade gives you the capability to turn ANY design or any font into a Rhinestone design very easily.

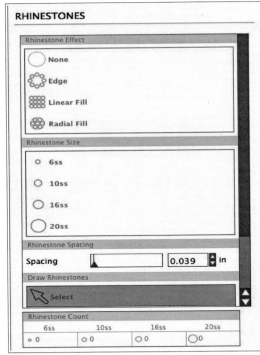

Find a design that you want to turn into a rhinestone template either from your library or imported and traced.

To turn cut lines into a rhinestone template simply select the design and click on the 'Open the Rhinestone Window' icon (X) along the top tool bar. Clicking on the icon brings up this window with lots of different options.

Depending on what you want your rhinestone design to look like select either edge, linear fill or radial fill.

Then you can decide on the rhinestone size. Your design will stay the same if you pick different size rhinestone you'll just have fewer actual rhinestones if you pick a larger size and more if you pick a smaller size.

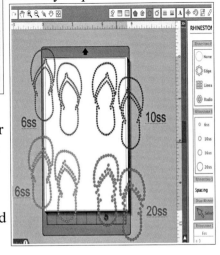
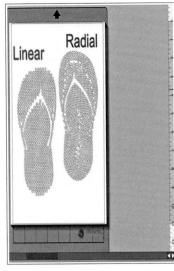

If the rhinestones are not spaced to your liking you can move them further apart or closer together using the spacing slider bar.

If after the rhinestones have been spread apart, some of the rhinestones seem to be out of place, you can move them manually by clicking the 'Release Rhinestones' option. This gives each rhinestone it's own selection box and allows you to move independently from using the arrow keys or mouse.

By using the 'single click' function you can add single rhinestones or use the free hand rhinestone tool to get a trail of rhinestones.

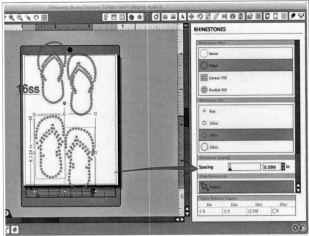

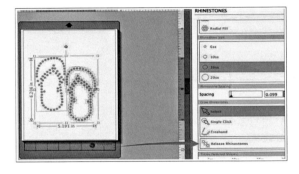

Stamps

Supplies: Stamping Material, Silhouette Stamp Mat, Blocks, Mounting foam

Recommended Retailers: Amazon

The Silhouette SD, Portrait and CAMEO can all cut stamps. You do, however, need the special stamp mat (which is smaller than both the CAMEO and Portrait mat, but will work in both).

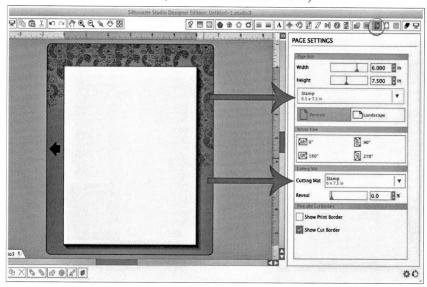

To get started, open up Silhouette Studio. Before you even start working with a design or shape, go to the Page Settings tool and from the drop down menu, select 'Stamp' 6.5 x 7.5 inches.

Slightly further down in the window, you'll also want to change the Cutting Mat to indicate that you are using the Stamp Mat. This is available in the drop down menu. Now your work area should show the stamping mat rather than the regular cutting mat.

Simple designs and/or ones that are welded are going to work best for stamps.

Once your design is ready, you'll want to size it. Keep in mind the size of the stamp, block, and ink pad. Position it on the mat in the software and now it's time to get ready to cut.

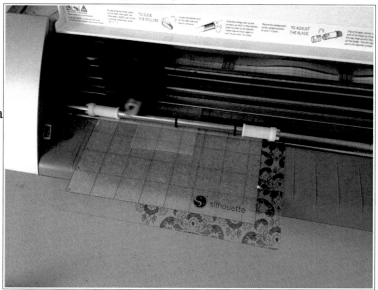

Peel off the white liner from your the stamp mat. Don't throw it away, you'll want to use it again to keep your mat clean.

Working with a single piece of the stamp material, keep the liner on it while you cut a piece that's just large enough for your stamp. If your design is 3"x3" for example, give yourself a little room and cut a 4"x4" square, instead of putting the entire sheet of stamp material on your cutting mat.

After the stamp material is cut to size, remove the liner.

Place the stamp material onto your mat

using the grids on the mat and in the software to arrange the material so the stamp cuts on the mat. Do not stretch or pull the stamp material. Just lay it down flat, gently rubbing out any bubbles.

> *TIP: Place the stamp material and the design in the center of the mat so they clear the rollers. This helps prevent the stamp material from bunching while cutting.*

From the Cut Settings window (o) pick 'Stamp Material' from the materials list. Don't forget to change your blade!!! You'll need to boost it to a 9.

On a CAMEO you'll need to move the right roller in towards the center. Flip up the blue lever on the right side. Pinch the roller with one hand, while holder the silver bar with the other and twist until the roller's teeth release from the notches. Slide the roller towards the center and lock it into place. Put the lever back down.

Load the mat and send the stamp design to the machine as you normally would.

When the cut is complete, unload the mat from the machine and using your fingers to gently 'weed' the excess stamp material away. Some areas probably didn't cut completely through and that's okay. Just pull it gently and the stamp material will snap.

Now you're left with your design - in a stamp form - on the mat.

If you have the starter kit, find the acrylic block that fits best and hand place the stamp to the block. To mount the stamps on a block of wood, use a mounting foam, such as EZ Cling Mounting Foam, which has an adhesive on one side to stick to a wood block.

Fabric

Recommended Tools: Fabric Blade, Silhouette Interfacing or Heat and Bond

Recommended Retailers: Amazon, Joann Fabrics, Walmart

Cutting Fabric with the Silhouette opens up a whole new world of crafting for sewers – especially applique. Instead of cutting the pieces of fabric out by hand, the machine can do all the hard work for you.

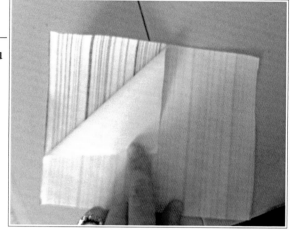

Design a fabric cut just like any other in Silhouette Studio – by either opening a design or typing out a line of text. You can even import embroidery designs by first converting them to a file type that Silhouette Studio can open: SVG, JPEG, PNG or PDF.

Once the design has been sized, according to the surface where it will be placed, select it. Take note of the dimensions. Cut a piece of fabric that is at least an inch longer and wider than the design. Iron the fabric to get out any wrinkles.

Cut a piece of interfacing so it fits over the entire piece of fabric and adhere it with an iron or heat press. It only takes 2 or 3 seconds to apply the interfacing to the fabric. The interfacing serves to stabilize and stiffen the fabric slightly as it's being cut.

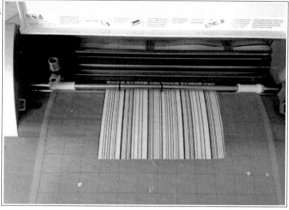

If necessary, trim down the fabric to the size of the interfacing.

Peel off the paper backing of the interfacing.

Place the fabric piece, on the cutting mat. If possible, place the fabric on the mat so it clears the rollers. This will help prevent the fabric from pulling up off the mat or getting jammed/wrinkled while cutting.

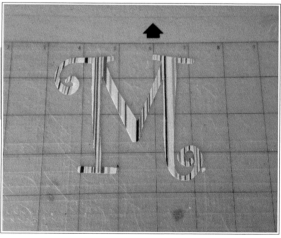

TIP: Be sure to check that the design on the virtual cutting mat in Silhouette Studio is in the same grid boxes as the fabric is on the cutting mat. Move the design, if necessary

From the material list in the Cut Style window (o) pick the type of fabric that's being cut. In this case, it's thin cotton fabric.

Remove the regular blade and replace it with a fabric blade, which should have been adjusted to the recommended depth. The blades are actually the same with the exception of the color of the case. This serves as a reminder for which blade should be kept exclusive to fabric.

From Silhouette Studio, send the fabric to cut.

Remove the excess fabric around the cut piece of fabric.

Since the interfacing is on the back of the design still, it can be temporarily adhered to another fabric surface with an iron or heat press so that it can more easily be sewn into place.

Cutting Fabric Patterns with PixScan

Combining Silhouette's PixScan technology with cutting fabric, is a powerful way to take fabric designs and appliques to the next level. The precision of PixScan allows Silhouette users to cut out a part of a pattern extremely easily. (See more in the PixScan chapter on Page 104)

Prepare the piece of fabric with the interfacing as described above. Place the fabric, with the interfacing on it onto the PixScan mat, ensuring the entire piece of fabric is within the boundary. Snap a photo of the entire Pixscan mat.

Upload the photo onto your computer and from Silhouette Studio click the PixScan icon (C). A window will open along the right side where you can "Import from File."

Click "Import PixScan Image from File." Navigate to the image on your computer and click 'OPEN'.

The photo will replace the image of that PixScan mat shown in the window as it loads into the software.

Once it's into Studio, the image will open in the work area.

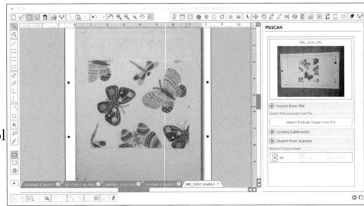

At this point you're going to use the Trace tool (k) to trace the section of the fabric that you want cut. Since it's like you only want to cut the edge, click "Trace Edge".

TIP: If areas were traced that you do not want to cut, select the trace > right click > release compound path > delete unwanted areas.

Here's a close up of the cut lines around the two butterflies that were traced and that will be cut.

Load the PixScan mat into the Silhouette as you normally would. Be sure to replace the regular blade with the fabric blade before cutting.

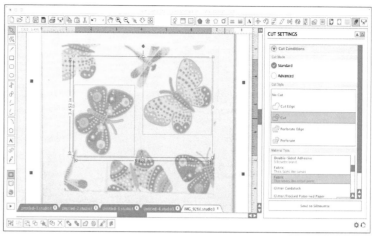

When the machine is finished cutting, you'll be left with an amazingly precise cut of only the area you wanted cut. This can then be used as an applique or however you choose to use it.

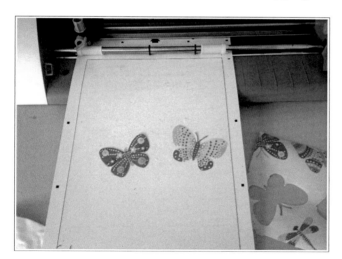

Engraving

Recommended Tools: Amy Chomas Engraving Tip

Retailers: AmyChomas.com, Amazon

With a special engraving tool it is possible for the Silhouette to engrave. Silhouette does not offer an engraving tool, but Amy Chomas Creations has an engraving tip that fits right into the machine.

Once you have the engraving tool you will obviously need a material to engrave on. It's important to keep in mind that the engraving tip does not produce a very deep etch. This has more to do with the pressure that can be applied by the Silhouette, than it does with the quality of the engraving tip.

The material that is being etched needs to be thick enough to produce a deep enough engraving, but not too thick that it won't fit under the rollers. Thin metal sheets, acrylic plastic sheets, c r and Core'dinations card stock, and blank stamping rounds are all engrave-able.

If you are engraving on a large area, the material can be placed onto the regular Silhouette cutting mat – as long as the mat is fairly sticky.

If engraving small charms or discs a PixScan mat is extremely helpful. Remember the beauty of PixScan is that it's super precise. Trying to accurately line up a small disc with the grids on the regular cutting mat is nearly impossible if you want the design centered on a disc that's half inch in diameter.

In order to get a deep engraving, it's necessary to add as much pressure to the tip as possible, as well as repeatedly double cut. Making two duplicates of the design and layering them on top of each other in Silhouette Studio and then clicking double cut will result in four rounds of engraving, for instance. To ensure that all of the copies of the design are perfectly aligned select them all at the same time and from the Align window click "Center." It will appear as if there is only one design, but really you have multiple copies stacked on top of each other. After you have stacked them, group the layers so they stay perfectly aligned.

When you're ready to cut, open up the Cut Settings window (o). Since Silhouette America doesn't make an engraver, there's no default settings. Use the Coverstock settings which put the thickness at 33 and the speed at a 1. The thickness is important because the thicker the material the more pressure that is put on the blade, or in this case, the engraver. You don't need to worry about the blade because you're going to replace it with the engraver.

After you pick Coverstock, you'll get a second scroll bar. Scroll down and check the box to double cut.

Load the mat into the machine and replace the blade with the Chomas Creations Engraver Tip and send the design to be cut.

Troubleshooting

Cutting Mat Issues

Is my machine supposed to be etching lines on my mat?

It is not uncommon for the blade to etch through the material making lines on the cutting mat. As long as the mat is not being cut through, and you are following the recommended cut settings, there is no need to worry.

Why is the material shifting on the mat while the Silhouette is cutting?

Material can shift while cutting on the Silhouette cutting mat, when the mat is not sticky enough to hold the material firmly in place during cutting. All cutting mats lose their stick over time. Certain materials can cause the mat to lose its stick more quickly than others.

Keeping the cutting mat free of dust and dirt can help extend its use. Always cover the cutting mat with the blue cover sheet when it's not in use. Also, avoid touching the sticky area of the cutting mat unnecessarily.

I can't cleanly lift the material off the mat and it's ruining my paper/vinyl.

This typically happens with new cutting mats. If paper and vinyl, specifically, are not easily able to be lifted off the mat cleanly, it's due to the mat being too sticky.

To take some of the sticky off a new mat blot it with a clean cotton shirt a few times. This should be enough to reduce the stick slightly so materials can be cleanly removed from the mat without ripping.

HELP! The mat is stuck in the machine.

If the cutting mat becomes stuck in the machine and absolutely will not budge do not pull it out! Follow these steps to remove the mat.

- Turn off the machine. Unplug the USB cable from the computer.
- Unplug the Silhouette's power cord from the outlet.
- Wait about a minute.
- Close out of Silhouette Studio to re-set everything (just be sure you save your project, first).
- Now work backwards. Start Silhouette Studio back up. Plug the power cord back into the wall. Plug the USB cable back into the computer. Finally turn the machine back on.
- Press the unload button and the mat should start being fed out.
- Continue pressing the unload button as many times as you need to to get the mat completely out of the machine.

Cutting Issues

Why is my machine not cutting or not cutting completely?

When the Silhouette is not cutting, or not cutting completely, it can be extremely frustrating. There are close to a dozen reasons why the Silhouette is not cutting. Check these issues out to troubleshoot:

- **No Blade** - Oops perhaps you forgot the blade altogether! Just put it in the slot, push it all the way down and turn the lock.

- **Blade is not down into the blade holder** - If the blade is not fully down into the blade holder it will not reach the material and therefore won't cut. You may also notice a clicking noise while cutting when the blade is not fully into the holder.

- **Blue Lock is not Locked** - Going right along with the blade not being fully in the holder, if the blade lock is not fully turned to the right to lock the blade into place, it will also cause the blade not to cut or not to cut correctly.

- **White Cap Not Screwed On** - If the white cap on the very end of the blade is not completely screwed on it will prevent the blade from reaching the material and therefore it cannot cut. Just give it a twist or two to screw it on until it's hand tight.

- **Blade Fin is Not Aligned at 6 o'clock** - The black fin on the blade housing must be pointed at the 6 o'clock position or cutting will not work correctly or at all. Unlock the blue lock and turn the blade until the fin is in the correct position.

- **Blade Obstructed** - If a piece of scrap material - usually vinyl or paper - is stuck on the blade it will cause cutting issues. Most common are incomplete cuts where some areas are cut, but other areas of the design are missed. Unscrew the white cap on the end of the blade to remove any lint or scraps that may be obstructing the blade.

- **No Cut Lines** - This is most often the root of cutting issues with SVG or imported images. If there are no cut lines around an image (indicated by "No Cut" in the Cut Style window (o)) the Silhouette doesn't know what to cut. Be sure you have thick red lines around your design. Go to the cut style window to turn on cut lines. If you are attempting to cut a JPEG or other image, you must trace the image first to get cut lines around it.

- **Wrong Settings** - The wrong cut settings can definitely be causing the Silhouette not to cut. For instance, if you are trying to cut card stock, but are using the vinyl settings, it's likely the blade won't even make a mark on the paper. Be sure to pick the correct medium from the material list in the cut style window and then adjust the blade accordingly. Remember, the thickness and speed are adjusted within the Silhouette Studio program, but you need to turn the blade to adjust the depth.

- **Interference** - If the Silhouette is making a tapping motion when you send it to cut it is most likely caused by interference from a wireless device nearby - most often a wireless printer. This could be a printer that's no longer in use, but still installed on the same computer you are using to cut with your Silhouette.

- **Silhouette Not Plugged In** – If the Silhouette is not powered on or not plugged in (either to a power outlet or into the USB port on your computer) it won't cut.

- **Mat and Material Not Loaded** - If the mat and material are not loaded they can't be cut.

Why is cutting starting above the gridded area of the cutting mat?

If the machine starts cutting too high or above the gridded area of the cutting mat, it's most likely that the "Load Media" is being used to load the mat into the machine rather than "Load Mat". Load Mat pulls the mat and material further into the machine and cutting starts lower to compensate for the margin area of the mat. Only use "Load Media" when cutting vinyl without a mat.

The blade is cutting a diagonal line back to the starting position.

The Silhouette Studio version (v3.3.437) had a software bug which caused the blade to cut a diagonal line from the last cut point to its "home base". Silhouette America released an update specifically to address this issue which includes a patch to repair the bug. Update to Silhouette Studio (3.3.451) or higher to fix the issue.

Blade, Tearing & Weeding Issues

I lost the ratchet to change the depth of my blade. How can I turn the blade?

Insert the blade into the built in ratchet on the front of the Silhouette machine and twist the blade to adjust the blade depth.

Why isn't the blade cutting completely through my material? I am having a difficult time weeding cleanly.

When the blade isn't cutting through the material completely, which can make weeding difficult, the cut settings need to be adjusted. Sometimes one blade depth is not deep enough, but just one setting up is too deep. Instead do one or both of the following one at a time to test if either works on its own. If not…do both:

1. In the cut settings, manually increase the thickness of the material. This puts more pressure on the blade so it pushes down harder as it cuts.

2. Double Cut

How can I stop the blade from tearing up the material as it cuts?

When cutting extremely thin designs, tearing from the blade is a common issue. To prevent the design from tearing add a very narrow offset around the design or text and cut the offset rather than the original. Most times an offset of .015 or .010 will be enough to satisfy the blade and get a clean cut.

If tearing continues to happen the pressure from the blade may be set too high. Reduce the thickness in the Cut Settings window (o). In addition, slow down the speed of the cut.

If none of the above work, it may be time to replace the blade. Try using a new blade and if the cutting issues resolve, you'll know the old blade was just too dull for a clean cut.

The cut line is 'off' or not completely cutting my design. Why and how do I fix it?

When the cut line does not meet up correctly, it's most often due to the material not staying in place as it's being cut. This can be caused by a mat that's not sticky enough to hold the material firmly in place.

How can I prevent the excess vinyl from sticking to itself as I weed?

If the excess vinyl is sticking to the vinyl design as you weed, it's likely to ruin a project. Add weeding lines in Silhouette Studio before cutting the project to make weeding easier and greatly reduce the risk of the vinyl sticking to itself.

Design Issues

Why can't I edit a font in my design?

If text has been edited in certain ways it's no longer considered text, but instead treated as a shape. Text that has been ungrouped, welded or had it's compound path released will no longer be editable as a font. This means the font style can't be changed.

I am unable to fill a shape with a solid color or pattern.

If the fill tools – fill color, fill gradient and fill pattern – are failing to fill a design, it is because the shape is not fully closed. This means the path as a break in it. Double click on the shape or click the edit points tools to view the shape's edit points (ee). The spot of the large red dot is where there is a break in the path. Double click it to have it connect with the other open end.

How do I turn off the drawing tools, knife and eraser? They are following me around the work area.

Hit 'Escape' on the keyboard to turn off the drawing tools, knife and eraser.

Silhouette Library & Software Troubleshooting

I purchased a design from the Silhouette Design Store, but it's not in my library.

If designs are not automatically downloading into your Silhouette Library, it could be because you have not registered your machine. Register your machine on the Silhouette America website and designs should begin to automatically download.

You can also go open up Silhouette Studio > File > Download Pending Orders.

I need to backup or move my entire library to another computer or hard drive. Can this be done without moving files one by one?

Yes. Simply click File > Export Library and follow the prompts.

To import the library to a new computer, install Silhouette Studio on the new computer. Sign in on the Silhouette America website/design store. Go to file > Import library.

I lost my Silhouette Studio software CD, how do I install the software?

The latest version of Silhouette Studio can be downloaded directly from the Silhouette America website.

I purchased the Silhouette Studio Designer Edition, but I don't know how to enter the key code.

Open up Silhouette Studio and click the Help menu. Select 'Activate License Key'. Follow the prompts.

Application Issues

My vinyl has bubbles. How can I get them out and prevent them?

Bubbles occur when air is trapped under the vinyl as it is applied to the surface. Burnish the bubbles, with a scraper or credit card, moving in the directly of the edge. Prick any bubbles remaining with a tiny pin and burnish again. Wait a few days, the bubbles will likely disappear.

You can prevent vinyl bubbles when applying by using the wet method to apply the vinyl. Applying the vinyl in a sort of rolling motion from the center up and then center down or top down, instead of putting the entire piece on all at once, can also help prevent bubbles.

How can I get vinyl straight on rounded surfaces?

To compensate for a rounded or conical surface, slightly curve the text in Silhouette Studio. Draw out a long oval using the Draw an Ellipse tool (ii) and place the text along the top to give it a slight curve. Putting the text on a path will help to compensate for the curve of the surface and keep the vinyl straight when applying to a tapered surface. Only text can be curved in this matter, designs can not be morphed. (See more on in the vinyl chapter.)

I have a hard time centering vinyl and stencils on the surface. Is there a fail-proof way to apply vinyl straight and centered?

Use the hinge method to apply vinyl and stencils to ensure they are straight, centered and even.

HTV Troubleshooting

My HTV is peeling up off the shirt I just made. How can I prevent this from happening?

There are many factors that can cause Heat Transfer Vinyl to peel up off a shirt. Go through the check list here to see where the issue is stemming from.

- The heat's too high

- The heat is not hot enough (check the manufacture's recommended temperature for application)

- Not enough pressure is being applied when using the iron to apply HTV

- The neck opening, a seam, buttons or snaps are creating a slight gap, preventing the heat press from getting a good seal on the HTV. Put a folded piece of cotton fabric or a mouse pad inside the shirt under the HTV to lift it up slightly and get a better seal.

- Shirt was not pre-pressed to remove moisture

- Shirt is not being washed inside out

- Shirt was put through the dryer

Peeling HTV can be fixed by putting a thin piece of cotton, such as a pillow case, over the HTV and applying more heat and pressure to re-adhere it.

How can I remove an HTV mistake?

Mistakes happen. Place a hot iron directly on the heat transfer vinyl and let it sit there for a few seconds. The HTV will start to melt right off the shirt. Depending on how well the HTV was adhered originally, the iron may need to sit on the HTV for up to a 30 seconds or a minute.

Print and Cut Troubleshooting

The Silhouette fails to detect the Registration Marks.

If the Silhouette is failing to find registration marks, there are a few different ways to fix this problem. Go through this checklist to troubleshoot.

- Did you remember to actually add registration marks before printing?

- Be sure the entire registration marks are actually being printed. Sometimes the printer will only print one side of the 90 degree registration mark. If this happens it won't be fully detected by the Silhouette. To fix this issue, move the registration marks up and/or in on the page from the 'Add Registration Marks' window.

If the registration marks are printed and are printed completely but are still not being detected, there are a few more things to check.

- Are the registration marks oriented and in the same position as they are in Silhouette Studio? Hold your paper exactly like you see it on the monitor and that's how you want to load it on the mat.

- Are you working in an area with low light? Flipping on an extra light or shining a flashlight on the registration marks can be enough to get the machine to find the registration marks.

- Is the paper or medium where the registration marks were printed heavily patterned? If the paper on which the registration marks were printed is patterned, it can be difficult for the machine to actually find the registration marks. Trace over the registration marks with a sharpie marker so they are more easily detected by the machine.

- Are you loading the mat correctly? If you load the mat too far to the left or right the machine may be looking in the wrong spot for the registration marks. This can cause it to fail when trying to detect the marks.

In addition, if you are "Loading Media" instead of "Loading Mat" the mat will not be pulled far enough into the machine and the Silhouette will have trouble finding the registration marks.

If your issue is that the machine is finding the registration marks, but not cutting along the edge of your design and is the same distance away from your design through the entire page you need to recalibrate the alignment.

The lines and/or text I added to my Print and Cut design are not printing.

If lines or text are part of your print and cut design, but they are not actually showing up when printed, the issue is that the line has no weight.

To fix this issue, select the lines to print and either go to the Line Style window (a) and give them a weight or select the lines to be printed and check the box "Print Lines of Selected Shapes" at the bottom of the Line Style window.

If text is not printing it's because it's either not filled or the unfilled text outline has no weight to it. Do one of the following to fix the issue and get the text to print.

To Fill With Solid Color
       a. Select the text > click the Fill tool (S) > pick a color
       b. Select the text > click the Line color tool (Z) > pick a color (to match the fill pick
          transparent or the exact same color using the color eye dropper)

To Fill With Solid Color
       a. Select the text > click the Fill tool (S) > pick a color
       b. Select the text > click the Line color tool (Z) > pick a color (to match the fill pick
          transparent or the exact same color using the color eye dropper)

The Silhouette is cutting what was only supposed to be printed on my Print and Cut design.

From Silhouette Studio, select everything you DO NOT want cut in the design. From the Cut Style window (o) click "No Cut". This will turn off the cut lines on these areas.

About the Author

Melissa Viscount is the founder, owner, and editor of Sihouette School blog. A SAHM to two young children, Melissa previously worked as a Television News Producer at three different NBC affiliates after graduating from Ithaca College. Following the birth of her oldest child in 2008, she stopped working outside the home to stay home and raise her children.

During that time, Melissa started her first blog, New Mama's Corner. She later added freelance writing to the mix working for both eHow.com and Examiner where she wrote on a wide variety of topics. In April 2013 Melissa started Two It Yourself, a DIY website where she and her sister shared DIY projects and tutorials.

In December 2013 Melissa received a Silhouette Portrait for Christmas (later adding a CAMEO to the family, as well). Recognizing there was a need for beginner-focused tutorials and written instruction she started a sister site to 2IY and in January 2014 Silhouette School blog was born. Silhouette School immediately took off and has become a go-to source of information, tutorials, and project ideas for Silhouette users around the world.   With a very active blog and social media following Silhouette School has become Melissa's flagship site. Daily requests for printable tutorials in logical order has lead to the writing of The Ultimate Silhouette Guide.

Melissa lives in Delaware with her husband, Bob, and their two young children.

Alphabetical Index

Made in the USA
San Bernardino, CA
23 February 2016